ISEE (Upper) Verbal Reasoning Sentence Completion and Synonyms

1000+ Practice Questions

by

K Williams

Copyright Notice

All rights reserved. Do not duplicate or redistribute in any form.

Table of Contents

Introduction to the Book 4

Sentence Completion: 7 Key Steps 5

   7 Key Steps in Action… 7

Sentence Completion 1 Blank Practice Set 1-12 13

Sentence Completion 2 Blank Practice Set 1-12 37

   Sentence Completion (1 Blank) Answers 61

   Detailed Explanations (1Blank) Set 1-5 62

   Sentence Completion (2 Blanks) Answers 72

   Detailed Explanations (2 Blanks) Set 1-5 73

Synonym Strategies 84

Synonyms Practice Set 1 - 30 95

   Synonyms - Answers 155

Introduction to the Book

The ISEE has a Verbal Reasoning section that is composed of two different kinds of questions:

Synonyms and Sentence Completions.

Both kinds of questions test your vocabulary and reasoning ability.

Synonym questions focus on word recognition, since the correct answer choices are those that have the same meaning, or are closest in meaning, to the word in the question. Synonyms also test your ability to reason, because you must choose the word that is most nearly the same in meaning to the word in the question from among four answer choices.

Sentence completion questions measure your ability to understand words and their function. Correct answers are based on clues that appear in the context of the sentence.

In the Upper Level forms of the ISEE, the sentence completion answer choices are **words or pairs of words** that logically complete the meaning of the sentence as a whole.

You have 17.5 minutes to answer 35 questions, and under time pressure, it is all too common to see students fumbling about with their sentences & their vocabulary, losing precious time.

What is needed is to be able to look at a problem, and have a A-ha, I have seen it before,

Moment!

And that is what this book will help you do.

This book will help you learn strategies to tackle the Verbal Reasoning section.

You will become well conversant with the steps to get to the correct answer, and you won't fumble even if you are not sure.

…..and with over 1000 practice questions, you will get a wide exposure to the different types of questions you may get in the exam, and you can face the actual test with assurance and confidence!

Sentence Completion: 7 Key Steps

A Sentence Completion question contains one or two blanks, to be filled in using the answer choices. These questions test your vocabulary and knowledge of the finer distinctions among words. A good vocabulary can be a great help here. But you can use many strategies for these questions, even without knowing the meaning of all the words.

The 7 Key Steps:

1. Read the Sentence

Use the sentence clues by reading the sentence thoroughly. Two things make a question difficult: difficult words and sentence structure. If you cannot dissect a sentence to figure out what fits best, you may not be able to answer the question even though you may know the meanings of all the words.

2. Hints

From reading the given sentence and the answer options carefully, you can sometimes get an idea of which word to use in the blanks.

Hence, you should look out for these 'hints' and help them guide you towards the correct answer.

An example below will illustrate the process;

Stepping out of the conference room to get some respite from the intensity of the _____, Reynolds wondered about the possible _____ of the merger on his personal life.

A. negotiations...ramifications
B. salutations...impact
C. meditations...repercussions
D. enumerations...consequences

In the above example, all the choices for the second blank have similar meanings, so the first blank has to be identified first. The hint that will help us do this is "merger". The event happening in the conference room is related to the "merger". Choices B, C, and D can be eliminated as a merger isn't saluted, meditated, or enumerated. A merger can only be negotiated. Thus Choice A is the correct answer.

3. Pluses and Minuses

Once you find the word clues, indicate the kind of word you're looking for with a + (positive meaning) or – (negative) sign.

4. Structure Words

Look for words like *but, rather, although, however, and, while, but, therefore, whereas*.

They reveal the sentence organization and tell you what kind of words to look for to complete the sentence accurately.

5. Punctuation

Analyze the sentence structure using the punctuation used like *colons, semicolons, commas and dashes*.

For complex and compound sentences, the punctuation used will help you get to the correct answer.

6. Visualize

Before you look at the answer choices, think of possible words that could be used to fill the blanks. If you know roughly the kind of words needed, the elimination is much easier. The word you visualize doesn't have to be fancy – a general idea is fine. This is better than trying out the choices to find out "what sounds good." It is faster and less prone to errors.

7. Plug-in answers

You can plug in the choices one by one to see if the sentence makes logical sense. This strategy often helps eliminate the more obviously wrong choices and lets you focus on fewer relevant choices.

When faced with an actual question, you will have to use one or more of the above strategies to arrive at the answer.

Let us work through a few examples and see how these strategies work for real ISEE questions.

7 Key Steps in Action…

Example 1:

Although the lives of the highest officials of the oppressive government are filled with luxury and _____, the general populace lives in terrible _____.

A. comfort…cruelty
B. splendor…poverty
C. anger…friendship
D. pain…joy

Step 1:

Read the sentence carefully and identify the structure. The use of the structure word *although* indicates that the sentence has a contradiction. The two blanks must have words that contrast with each other.

Step 2:

Choose which blank to solve first. The second blank is part of a smaller phrase "*the general populace lives in terrible_____*" and has an adjective describing it directly (*terrible*). So it should be easier to solve.

Step 3:

Identify if the second blank has a positive or negative connotation. Since the adjective describing it is negative (*terrible*), the noun word that fits will also be negative. Mark the blank with -ve sign.

Step 4:

Find the answer choices that have a negative word for the second blank. (C) and (D) have positive words and can be eliminated. So the choices are narrowed down to (A) and (B).

Step 5:

Plug in both the choices to see if which one fits better contextually. The second blank is about the life of people.. *terrible cruelty* is a quality possessed by humans and not a quality of living. Thus (A) doesn't make sense contextually in the second blank. *terrible poverty* shows how the people are living so (B) is the correct choice.

Step 6:

Confirm your answer by plugging in the first blank. *Splendor* is a positive word that fits the phrase *luxury and splendor* and aptly describes how the highest officials of the government live. Thus you can confirm Choice (B) as the correct answer.

Example 2:

He is _____ speaker; his discourses are always informative and inspirational.

(A.) an eloquent
B. an amateur
C. a novice
D. an inarticulate

Step 1:

Visualize the sentence. It is talking about a speaker. The use of a semi-colon, shows that both parts of the sentence are reinforcing each other. The second part describes the speaker's *discourses* (speeches) positively. Thus the blank in the first part must also contain a positive word.

Step 2:

Identify the positive words in the options. This involves using your knowledge of vocabulary. An *amateur* is not a professional. It is a word with negative connotations. A *novice* is a beginner in any skill or profession. It is a negative word. An *inarticulate* person cannot speak well. It is a negative word too. Thus (B), (C), and (D) can be eliminated as they are negative words. Only (A) has a positive word - *eloquent* (fluent).

Step 3:

Plug-in (A) in the blank to confirm that it makes sense contextually. *He is an eloquent speaker; his discourses are always informative and inspirational* makes perfect sense. Hence (A) is the answer.

Example 3:

The _____ requirements by the client for approving new designs, do not _____ designers when it comes to research & development because of the profit potential.

A. wonderful...provoke
B. onerous...dissuade
C. complex...encourage
D. vague...support

Step 1:

Identify the most obvious hint. *because of the profit potential* that occurs at the end of the sentence is the reason for the rest of the sentence. It will help to fill the blanks. The hint shows that the designers are doing what they are doing because of the profit potential.

Step 2:

Fill the second blank. The second blank needs a verb to describe the action of the designers who are motivated by the profit potential. The action must be a positive word. Since there is a *not* before the blank, the blank itself should contain a negative word (double negative will become positive). (C) and (D) are positive words and can be eliminated. (A) and (B) are both negative words and can be used in the second blank.

Step 3:

Fill the first blank. The first blank requires a negative word as the requirements are supposed to either *provoke* or *dissuade* the designers but are countered by the profit potential. In (A) the first blank has a positive word *wonderful* - A wonderful requirement will neither *provoke* nor *dissuade* a designer; it would rather excite or motivate him. So (A) can be eliminated leaving (B) as the answer.

Step 4:

Plug-in the answer choice to see if the sentence makes logical sense. *The onerous requirements…do not dissuade designers…because of the profit potential* makes perfect sense.

Example 4:

The bicentennial anniversary of Mozart's death is being _____ around the world with concerts featuring his work.

A. liberated
B. commemorated
C. expatiated
D. protracted

This is a straight forward vocabulary knowledge question where the logical and structural strategies are of minimal help. The only way to answer these type of questions is to build up a good vocabulary knowledge base.

Step 1:

Identify the hint. All the answer choices are verbs. The blank must be an action that happens to an *anniversary*. So see which options you can eliminate with this hint.

Step 2:

Narrowing answer choices. (A) has the easiest word amongst the choices. It can be eliminated first as an anniversary cannot be *liberated*. (D) has another more common word *protracted* (prolonged). This too can be eliminated as an anniversary can't be prolonged.

Step 3:

Use vocabulary knowledge to arrive at the answer. *expatiate* means speak and *commemorate* means observe. An anniversary cannot be spoken, it can only be observed. Hence (B) is the correct answer.

Example 5:

A staunch advocate of impartiality in grading, the professor ensured that he assessed his students using _____ process.

A. a logical
B. an arbitrary
C. a meticulous
D. a disinterested

Some questions have one or more options that can potentially fill the blank. Such questions need a careful study of the context to eliminate the trap answer choices.

Step 1:

Visualize the question and identify the hint. The question describes a professor and his way of assessing students. The professor is described as an *advocate of impartiality in grading*. This tells us that his grading process must be impartial and fair. The blank must be filled with an answer choice that is closest to this meaning.

Step 2:

Identifying the answer choice that is the best fit. (B) can be eliminated immediately as it means the opposite of fair. (A), (C), and (D) all three can theoretically fit in the blank.

You need to find the best fit from these three.

Meticulous means careful. A careful assessment need not be impartial or fair. So (C) can be eliminated.

Similarly a *logical* assessment need not be impartial or fair and (A) can also be eliminated.

This leaves us with *disinterested* (meaning unbiased).

This fits best as a disinterested assessor won't bring his prejudices into grading and will be impartial.

Example 6:

American hero and Civil War general Ulysses S. Grant harbored social anxiety so severe that he even refused to make an appearance at his daughter's wedding. Yet, in the most critical of moments, he was _____ both in mind and demeanor.

A. mercurial
B. pleasant
C. frank
D. composed

Some questions contain long sentences with convoluted structure and sometimes even more than one sentence. To tackle such questions, you need to reread the sentence a few times to get a clear understanding of what the sentence is about before attempting to answer it.

Step 1:

Reread the first sentence a few times to get a clear understanding of what it says. - General Grant was a shy person. He did not attend even his daughter's wedding. The second sentence begins with a contrasting conjunction "yet", so it is describing a scenario opposite to what the first sentence described. General Grant was not shy or anxious during critical moments.

Step 2:

Narrow the answer choices to fit the sentence. The blank must be filled with an adjective that is the opposite of anxious and shy. Of all the answer choices, (D) *composed* is the only one that comes closest to the meaning.

Now, you can apply your learning from the previous pages to solve the following sentence completion questions quickly and accurately.

Sentence Completion 1 Blank Practice Set 1-12

SENTENCE COMPLETION SET 1

1. It is ironic and somehow tragic that good people are often dull while evil people can be endlessly _____.

   A) ordinary
   B) stubborn
   C) skeptical
   D) fascinating

2. Extremist advocates of the occult claim that existing systems of scientific thought must at least be modified, if not _____.

   A) evaluated
   B) supplemented
   C) incorporated
   D) overturned

3. There is some _____ the fact that the author of a book as sensitive and informed as Indian Artisans did not develop her interest in Native American art until adulthood, for she grew up in a region rich in American Indian.

   A) irony in
   B) satisfaction in
   C) doubt about
   D) concern about

4. Although adolescent, maturational and developmental states occur in an orderly sequence, their timing _____ with regard to onset and duration.

   A) lasts
   B) varies
   C) falters
   D) accelerates

5. Although the substance is normally quite _____, scientists found that when tempered with other elements it could be stored safely in metal containers.

   A) voluminous
   B) caustic
   C) insoluble
   D) vapid

6. Amid the collapsing or out-of-control mechanical devices, the belching volcano had a disturbingly _____ quality, like a character who has stumbled on-stage by mistake.

A) anomalous
B) vacant
C) obdurate
D) derelict

7. Far from being mere replicas of seventeenth-century African culture, Maroon societies have continually developed as their members have _____ the artistic heritage bequeathed by their ancestors, adapting it creatively to their changing lives.

A) confused
B) invented
C) repressed
D) modified

8. The English novelist William Thackeray considered the cult of the criminal so dangerous that he criticized Dickens' Oliver Twist for making the characters in the thieves' kitchen so _____.

A) threatening
B) riveting
C) conniving
D) fearsome

9. The ambassador's papers are not _____ reading, but one who reads slowly and attentively will be richly repaid.

A) petty
B) valuable
C) insightful
D) easy

10. Philosophical problems arise when people ask questions that, though very _____, have certain characteristics in common.

A) relevant
B) elementary
C) abstract
D) diverse

SENTENCE COMPLETION SET 2

1. Because he felt intimidated in his new position, he was _____ divulging his frank opinions of company proposals.

   A) scurrilous about
   B) candid in ✓
   C) chary of
   D) fervid about

2. By forcing our surrender to the authority of the clock, systematic timekeeping has imposed a form of _____ on society.

   A) anarchy
   B) permanence
   C) provincialism
   D) tyranny ✓

3. After the war, the consumer demand that had been repressed by war priorities _____ the defense effort as a stimulus to industry.

   A) included
   B) replaced
   C) released
   D) aroused ✓

4. Kagan maintains that an infant's reactions to its first stressful experience are part of a natural process of development, not harbingers of childhood unhappiness or _____ signs of adolescent anxiety.

   A) prophetic ✓
   B) normal
   C) monotonous
   D) virtual

5. Scholars' sense of the uniqueness of the central concept of "the state" at the time when political science became an academic field quite naturally led to striving for a correspondingly _____ mode of study.

   A) thorough
   B) distinctive ✓
   C) dependable
   D) scientific

6. Nutritionists declare that the mineral selenium, despite its toxic aspects, is _____ to life, although it is needed only in extremely small quantity.

A) destructive
B) insignificant
C) essential
D) extraneous

7. Before the 1930's, the knowledge one could give their children would last them their working lives, whereas today the technological revolution often renders familiar scientific developments _____ overnight.

A) valid
B) expedient
C) obsolete
D) immortal

8. Certainly Murray's preoccupation with the task of editing the Oxford English Dictionary begot a kind of monomania, but it must be regarded as a _____ or at least an innocuous one.

A) tame
B) tendentious
C) meretricious
D) beneficent

9. Scientists have always recognized that deforestation will have an impact on the immediate environment but they now warn that cutting down large forests can _____ problems on a much wider scale.

A) generate
B) isolate
C) disturb
D) curtail

10. Ecology, like economics, concerns itself with the movement of valuable _____ through a complex network of producers and consumers.

A) commodities
B) dividends
C) communications
D) nutrients

SENTENCE COMPLETION SET 3

1. The committee warned that if its suggestions were not implemented, the problems would be _____ and eventually rendered insoluble.

   A) exacerbated
   B) insurmountable ✓
   C) obliterated
   D) vindicated

2. Some scientists argue that carbon compounds play such a central role in life on Earth because of the possibility of _____ resulting from the carbon atom's ability to form an unending series of different molecules.

   A) deviation
   B) stability
   C) reproduction ✓
   D) variety

3. We first became aware that her support for the new program was less than _____ when she declined to make a speech in its favor.

   A) qualified
   B) haphazard
   C) fleeting
   D) wholehearted ✓

4. Carlos Saura is not given to explicit statement; his films, which seem hazy because of their psychological _____, often leave the uninitiated puzzled and unmoved.

   A) causality ✓
   B) poignancy
   C) conditioning
   D) allusiveness

5. The spellings of many Old English words have been _____ in the living language, although their pronunciations have changed.

   A) preserved ✓
   B) shortened
   C) preempted
   D) revised

6. Current data suggest that, although _____ states between fear and aggression exist, fear and aggression are as distinct physiologically as they are psychologically.

A) simultaneous
B) serious
C) exceptional
D) transitional

7. The self-important cant of musicologists on record jackets often suggests that true appreciation of the music is an _____ process closed to the uninitiated listener, however enthusiastic.

A) unreliable
B) arcane
C) arrogant
D) elementary

8. Wildlife represents a renewable resource but one that cannot be _____ for the enjoyment of future generations.

A) replaced
B) stockpiled
C) balanced
D) withdrawn

9. Students who interpret the honor code strictly find it _____ that some bright students complete take-home examinations for less proficient friends.

A) remedial
B) irreproachable
C) unconscionable
D) irrelevant

10. In order to be sold to worldwide television, a movie should be _____; that is, it should neither use strong language nor tackle a controversial theme.

A) didactic
B) innocuous
C) illustrative
D) derivative

SENTENCE COMPLETION SET 4

1. Until the current warming trend exceeds the range of normal climatic fluctuations, there will be, among scientists, considerable _____ the possibility that increasing levels of atmospheric C02 can cause long-term warming effects.

   A) interest in
   B) uncertainty about
   C) enthusiasm for
   D) worry about

2. It has been argued that politics as _____, whatever its transcendental claims, has always been the systematic organization of common hatreds.

   A) a theory
   B) an ideal
   C) a practice
   D) a contest

3. Within the tribal government of the Crow Indians, the clan system serves as a method of checks and balances that _____ the assumption of authoritarian rule by any one clan.

   A) determines
   B) prevents
   C) examines
   D) delegates

4. The public politician and the private person were _____; this mayor was no more and no less than she appeared to be.

   A) impervious
   B) invincible
   C) inscrutable
   D) indivisible

5. He was widely regarded as a _____ man because he revealed daily his distrust of human nature and human motives.

   A) disrespectful
   B) cynical
   C) confused
   D) misinformed

6. He is an unbeliever, but he is broad-minded enough to decline the mysteries of religion without _____ them.

A) denouncing
B) understanding
C) praising
D) doubting

7. Dreams are _____ in and of themselves, but, when combined with other data, they can tell us much about the dreamer.

A) uninformative
B) starting
C) harmless
D) unregulated

8. Because modern scientists find the ancient Greek view of the cosmos outdated and irrelevant, they now perceive it as only of _____ interest.

A) historical
B) intrinsic
C) astronomical
D) experimental

9. The job allowed no relaxation, but Joan enjoyed _____ and welcomed the challenge of dealing with the variety of problems that came across her desk every day.

A) leisure
B) monotony
C) pressure
D) privacy

10. A common argument claims that in folk art, the artist's subordination of technical mastery to intense feeling _____ the direct communication of emotion to the viewer.

A) facilitates
B) averts
C) neutralizes
D) implies

SENTENCE COMPLETION SET 5

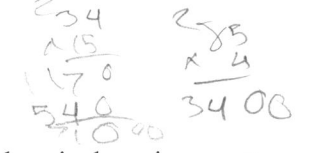

1. The increasing frequency of bee colony collapses across the northern hemisphere is a matter of _____ concern given our dependence on bee-pollinated agriculture.

   A) conventional
   B) immaterial
   C) grave
   D) tendentious

2. The annual Memorial Day parade, which is usually a _____ affair, has been turned into a vulgar spectacle by the town council this year.

   A) murky
   B) adulterous
   C) solemn
   D) clandestine

3. While the colonial administration was occupied with putting down the Zulu rebellion in the North, firebrand Boer politicians were _____ trouble in the southern cities.

   A) collaborating
   B) designing
   C) fomenting
   D) conducting

4. "This man can easily beat a lie detector", remarked the policeman "In my twenty seven years of service I have never met anyone who can _____ this easily".

   A) interrogate
   B) apprehend
   C) denounce
   D) dissemble — conceal one's truths

5. Ulysses S. Grant was a man of few words and an exception to the rule that successful American presidential candidates can't be _____.

   A) inarticulate
   B) gregarious
   C) convivial
   D) loquacious

6. In the 20th century the labor movement has succeeded in passing legislation in several countries to _____ the condition of the working classes.

A) enervate
B) ameliorate
C) abridge
D) abdicate

7. The police managed to _____ the masked robbers after a tense stand-off that lasted nearly 36 hours and was widely televised all over the state.

A) comprehend
B) apprehend
C) dedicate
D) cadge

8. For over a hundred years, the central banks' attempts to replace the gold-standard have been _____ by the lack of an alternative asset class that has all the advantages of the yellow metal.

A) assuaged
B) abrogated
C) hindered
D) glistened

9. The commission investigating the Old town riots of 2019 has concluded that the _____ were not local and must have been criminal elements intent on spreading chaos in the neighborhood.

A) negotiators
B) corporators
C) proposers
D) instigators

10. Since Mark doesn't bother to hide his _____ for the new management anymore, it is obvious he doesn't plan to continue working here for long.

A) disdain
B) admiration
C) sycophancy
D) consideration

SENTENCE COMPLETION SET 6

1. A large part of the criminal justice code in the commonwealth countries was originally written to suit the socio-economic conditions _____ in late 19th century Britain.

   A) prudent
   B) congruent
   C) attendant
   D) prevalent

2. A young Pierre Curie used to cycle twenty kilometers every day to the university library so that he could _____ his hunger for knowledge.

   A) ingratiate
   B) satiate
   C) delicate
   D) obdurate

3. Shakespeare portrays Lady Macbeth as someone whose soul is deeply _____ with avarice and jealousy.

   A) painted
   B) anointed
   C) tainted
   D) planted

4. Though the Japanese ended their policy of isolation and started trading with European nations, the country continued to remain _____ to westerners for many decades to come.

   A) a cornucopia
   B) an amphora
   C) a satellite
   D) an enigma

5. It was not until recently that the tobacco industry stopped its opposition to funding studies on the _____ health effects of the chemical compounds in cigarettes.

   A) detrimental
   B) incremental
   C) illusionary
   D) anachronistic

6. The least we can do for the patients undergoing chemotherapy is being _____ enough not to comment on the changes in their physical appearance.

A) considerate
B) egregious
C) lucid
D) rigorous

7. The Iditarod trail race is considered to be the greatest endurance race in sport history not only because of its grueling nature but also because of the _____ landscape across which it takes place.

A) pandemic
B) desolate
C) paradoxical
D) intransigent

8. The city's vaunted walls withstood countless attacks through the centuries only to be breached during the siege of 1453, when a group of _____ guards opened the gates to the besiegers.

A) ambivalent
B) germane
C) treacherous
D) succulent

9. The reconciliatory policies of Mandela's first administration were intended to _____ the horrors of Apartheid and heal the nation.

A) quench
B) exaggerate
C) exacerbate
D) mitigate

10. The Berlin Conference of 1875, was an attempt by the competing colonial powers to _____ the mess of African colonization and bring about a permanent agreement.

A) absolve
B) placate
C) denounce
D) untangle

SENTENCE COMPLETION SET 7

1. It came as a surprise to Watson, when Adler dropped her normal _____ demeanor and started bickering with Moriarty as if she were haggling with a fishmonger.

   A) congenital
   B) congenial
   C) gargantuan
   D) ephemeral

2. By _____ the well-known ferocity of the guard dog with the fact that it reportedly did not bark at all on the night of the murder, Holmes deduced that the murderer was someone familiar to it.

   A) genuflecting
   B) juxtaposing
   C) conniving
   D) intervening

3. It is frustrating for new parents when their easy-going baby suddenly becomes a _____ toddler whose food preferences are very limited.

   A) somnolent
   B) hedonistic
   C) finicky
   D) ethereal

4. The flames soon reached the gunpowder magazine of HMS *Hood* and the resulting explosion _____ the once mighty battlecruiser with a wreath of smoke and fire.

   A) caressed
   B) slinked
   C) exposed
   D) engulfed

5. While it may be _____ for researchers to not publish the studies that don't produce expected results, the practice severely affects future research in related areas.

   A) expedient
   B) eligible
   C) caustic
   D) unambiguous

6. Despite their fabled martial arts skills, the warrior monks of the Shaolin temple never served in armies as they had to _____ all forms of violence.

A) discern

B) forswear ✓

C) contend

D) leverage

7. Given the _____ manner in which the policy was implemented, it is natural to see it beset with chaos and controversy.

A) strategic

B) salutary

C) fastidious

D) haphazard

8. Revere's midnight ride that warned the American forces about the _____ British invasion was immortalized by H. W. Longfellow in the 1860 poem *Paul Revere's Ride*.

A) imminent ✓

B) eminent

C) eminent

D) immigrant

9. The Alcatraz maximum security prison, popularly known as "The Rock", was originally built to incarcerate the most _____ prisoners in the state of California.

A) placid

B) incorrigible

C) veritable

D) vapid

10. Since 2003, the Scandinavian countries have not only taken in nearly a million refugees from the world's conflict zones, but also have managed to successfully _____ them into their societies.

A) insinuate ✓

B) upskill

C) integrate

D) eliminate

SENTENCE COMPLETION SET 8

1. The oppressive Indian summer, when the mercury soars very high, makes people _____ and dazed especially during the afternoons.

   A) zestful
   B) devious
   C) traditional
   D) languid

2. It has taken nearly two decades of research and repeated warnings from scientists to make the wider public aware of the _____ influence TV commercials have on young children.

   A) impecunious
   B) nonchalant
   C) maleficent
   D) impudent

3. _____ vegetation growing around Chernobyl attest to the long lasting nature of radiation poisoning effects caused by the old Soviet reactor's meltdown.

   A) enumerated
   B) malformed
   C) indignant
   D) downcast

4. After the death of Tito, the Yugoslav republic split into a _____ of factions that soon started a decade-long vicious civil war.

   A) multiplicity
   B) hubris
   C) amalgamation
   D) quandary

5. By 1936, the power of the parliament had eroded completely leaving the office of the president _____ and answerable to no one.

   A) oblivious
   B) indelicate
   C) harrowing
   D) omnipotent

6. Though a vast majority of Vermeer's subjects are from the lower classes, he portrayed them with extraordinary _____ and dignity - a technique other painters of his era reserved only for the portraits of nobility.

A) poise
B) indolent
C) inertia
D) appetite

7. The _____ with which the health department's pandemic response teams reacted to the outbreak shows that they had been anticipating it for some time now.

A) ennui
(B) promptness
C) skepticism
D) revelry

8. The weakening of labor rights and dilution of corporate governance standards have aided the _____ corporate raiders to take over scores of medium sized companies easily.

A) penitent
B) indigent
C) rapacious
D) infallible

9. The great Emperor is still _____ as a great ruler not on account of his valor and conquests but because of his wisdom and compassion for his subjects.

(A) reviewed
B) relinquished
C) adjured
D) revered

10. Reaves is a rarity among Hollywood celebrities - a reclusive, _____ man whose acts of kindness towards strangers have turned him into a legend.

A) self-effacing
B) accurate
C) antagonistic
D) miserly

SENTENCE COMPLETION SET 9

1. Though the state governments are nominally _____ to the federal government, in practice most of them function with a great deal of autonomy.

   A) subjugate
   B) pertinent
   C) superfluous
   D) subordinate

2. Coca Cola's domination of the soft drinks segment became _____ after the failure of New Coke in the 1980s and was eventually ended by the emergence of Pepsi as the new market leader.

   A) tenacious
   B) conceited
   C) tentative
   D) inoperable

3. Philip V took _____ at the increasing privateer attacks on the treasure galleons and threatened to launch a second armada against the British Isles in retaliation.

   A) chagrin
   B) umbrage
   C) euphoria
   D) contentment

4. Zuleika Dobson was a _____ girl who quickly became popular amongst both the students and teachers of Oxford.

   A) vivacious
   B) hallowed
   C) expansive
   D) curmudgeonly

5. Much of the Victorian era poems are _____ in nature and employ a wide range of allusions and metaphors to convey their message.

   A) inimical
   B) cardinal
   C) primordial
   D) allegorical

6. Germany's demands for control of the Polish corridor barely a year after the signing of the Munich Agreement revealed how wrong Chamberlain was to try and _____ Hitler by ceding control of Czechoslovakia.

A) anoint
B) hegemonize
C) appease
D) equivocate

7. The San Francisco earthquake of 1906 and the resultant loss of life revealed how _____ the state of California had grown about disaster mitigation.

A) masterly
B) complacent
C) deceitful
D) incongruent

8. The _____ of social democracy is leveling the playing field and bringing about equality of opportunity for all sections of society.

A) crux
B) bane
C) hoax
D) pillage

9. Eppie grew up to be a talkative and _____ young woman, in stark contrast to her shy and reclusive adoptive father.

A) reticent
B) discontent
C) fatalistic
D) ebullient

10. In times of recession, Keynes recommends that government _____ should go up to make up for the lack of investments from the private sector.

A) supervision
B) regulation
C) expenditure
D) austerity

SENTENCE COMPLETION SET 10

1. The _____ shown by the town people in dealing with the destruction caused by Hurricane Sandy surprised and heartened the National guardsmen sent to rescue them.

   A) fortitude
   B) indolence
   C) annulment
   D) snarkiness

2. The Greek army's march through a thousand miles of hostile Persian territory was _____ by Xenophon in his epic Anabasis and is considered among the greatest adventures in human history.

   A) amortized
   (B) immortalized
   C) scrounged
   D) demoralized

3. The main challenge Piccard faced while designing the Trieste was to come up with a way to maintain hull _____ when the bathyscaphe was subjected to enormous pressures under water.

   A) integrity
   B) credibility
   (C) liquidation
   D) unfolding

4. Advancements in DNA technology offer hope to thousands of prisoners _____ in prisons having been convicted on flimsy grounds.

   A) thriving
   B) chartering
   C) adventuring
   (D) languishing

5. By the time the company realized what it was up against, the _____ disinformation campaign had driven its share price below the 10$ mark.

   A) mundane
   B) grueling
   (C) malicious
   D) epic

6. Darwin was preparing for a sedate and _____ life as a country priest, when he got the exciting news about an opening for a naturalist aboard HMS Beagle.

A) tumultuous
B) mundane ✓
C) sensational
D) atrocious

7. The East German state's iron grip on its populace was made possible by its _____ secret police - the Stasi - whose informants had infiltrated every section of society.

A) omnipresent
B) exasperating
C) indulgent
D) emancipated

8. A _____ Long John Silver paced the deck of the *Hisponiala*, planning his next move after his initial attempt to seize the treasure failed miserably.

A) plausible
B) predictable
C) ponderous ✓
D) pensive

9. Microsoft stopped the production of Windows phones and got out the mobile phone segment citing the _____ condition of the market dominated by Apple and Android devices.

A) placid
B) immodest
C) adverse ✓
D) colluding

10. The government spokesman became _____ when the media started questioning him about the corruption scandal and tried to change the subject.

A) exuberant
B) reticent
C) inundated
D) virulent

SENTENCE COMPLETION SET 11

1. I am afraid that the kids won't like the _____ life in the countryside after six years of getting used to the fast paced urban life.

   A) sedentary
   B) servile
   C) seminal
   D) statutory

2. The teacher suspected something was wrong as the class was uncharacteristically _____ throughout the day.

   A) irrigated
   B) subdued
   C) ambulatory
   D) kinetic

3. Galileo was persecuted and thrown into prison because he had the _____ to question the geocentric model of the universe endorsed by the catholic church.

   A) tribulation
   B) amiability
   C) temerity
   D) generosity

4. Professional swimmers and divers don't view swimsuits just as fashion accessories anymore and use them to enhance their _____ by preventing the buildup of lactic acid in their bodies.

   A) disorientation
   B) leverage
   C) reputation
   D) stamina

5. Accounts of contemporary historians and foreign travelers portray Suleiman the Magnificent as a _____ ruler who did not tolerate even a hint of dissent from his advisers and courtiers.

   A) tyrannical
   B) preposterous
   C) fecund
   D) nonchalant

6. The Black Death of the 14th century, generally considered to be the deadliest pandemic in human history was even more _____ than the Spanish flu of 1918.

A) vindictive
B) virulent
C) succulent
D) salubrious

7. The old king realized that his wayward sons were hurtling the country towards a/an _____ and decided to hand power over to the senate.

A) zenith
B) junction
C) abyss
D) crux

8. The cornerstone of any modern immigration policy should be the proactive measures to assimilate immigrants into the mainstream and prevent their _____ from society.

A) enactment
B) accompaniment
C) enumeration
D) alienation

9. People conveniently forget that the United States had its fair share of fascist _____ who advocated an isolationist foreign policy to prevent America from joining the anti-fascist coalition.

A) apologists
B) pedagogues
C) communes
D) ambushers

10. A major air catastrophe was _____ when an unusually alert air traffic controller at the La Guardia Airport discovered that the main radar system was malfunctioning and rebooted it in time to avoid several mid-air collisions.

A) advocated
B) averted
C) probated
D) assayed

SENTENCE COMPLETION SET 12

1. The magnitude of the crisis was so much so that even the usually _____ legal department meekly accepted the plan proposed by the Chief Financial Officer.

   A) congenital
   B) camaraderie
   C) combative
   D) oppressive ✓

2. The University budget did not have enough money for a new biology lab, but the professor managed to _____ a few thousand dollars from a private foundation and built it.

   A) tally
   B) bestow
   C) cavort
   D) cadge ✓

3. The main island in the archipelago _____ its name from the 18th century French explorer Louis Antoine de Bougainville who was the first European to set foot on it.

   A) derives ✓
   B) abhors
   C) rescinds
   D) accords

4. That Country's Army had the _____ distinction of being the only army to be soundly defeated in three successive wars within a century.

   A) laudable ✓
   B) dubious
   C) esoteric
   D) epileptic

5. Once tea cultivation took off in India, Europe was not dependent on the Chinese suppliers anymore and the _____ price of tea came down sharply.

   A) equivocal
   B) voluptuous
   C) exorbitant
   D) exhaustive

6. The entry of the United States into World War II in December 1941, made the outcome of the war a _____ conclusion.

A) preliminary
B) preemptive
C) foregone
D) volatile

7. From a big name director with a massive budget to an all-star cast and expensive marketing campaign, '*After Earth*' had almost everything needed for a blockbuster hit, but was done in by a _____ and uninspired script.

A) sky-rocketing
B) symmetrical
C) sibilant
D) hackneyed

8. If quantum computing becomes a reality, the strength of the encryption will become _____ as computers could crack it just by using their raw computing power.

A) immaterial
B) consequential
C) derogatory
D) obsolete

9. The headquarters of the hedge fund is situated at an _____ brown building in Hartford that can be mistaken for an accountant's office.

A) eclectic
B) unhinged
C) idolatry
D) inconspicuous

10. The summer of 2006 was the high tide of the _____ that saw dozens of bombings and ambushes that nearly cut off the capital from the rest of the country.

A) insurgency
B) armistice
C) maneuvers
D) climax

Sentence Completion 2 Blank Practice Set 1-12

SENTENCE COMPLETION SET 1

1. As a young man, Jean Toomer spoke of his desire to integrate the seemingly _____ elements of his racial heritage so that they might _____, rather than oppose, each other.

   A) archaic…reprove
   B) contrary…complement
   C) dissimilar… dispel
   D) baffling…exceed

2. Even those who _____ the aphorism "history repeats itself" must now _____ the fact that certain events bear marked resemblances to incidents of earlier history.

   A) reject … doubt
   B) deny… acknowledge
   C) defend…perceive
   D) ignore… forget

3. In a way, science might be described as _____ thinking applied to nature; we are looking for natural conspiracies, for connections among apparently _____ data.

   A) national ... hard
   B) imaginative ... original
   C) critical…inaccurate
   D) paranoid…disparate

4. "I support whatever actions my police chief takes," the mayor stated _____; now, however, with suits being brought against the police department, the mayor regrets having made such _____.

   A) prematurely…a qualification
   B) categorically … a denunciation
   C) initially ... an endorsement
   D) ambiguously... a resolution

5. Life during the depression era was too frightening to be portrayed _____; hence, most reviewers accepted escapist movies without _____.

   A) realistically… criticism
   B) objectively… consequence
   C) sentimentally… shame
   D) intelligently… thought

6. Scientists are studying the birth and growth of thunderstorms to discover what causes the difference between showers that enable crops to _____ and _____ storms that cause floods and erosion.

A) flourish…violent
B) wither…damaging
C) grow…harmless
D) parch…severe

7. The book's premise is that conventional measures of the economy's performance are _____ because they _____ social and environmental costs that are obviously important.

A) moribund…anticipate
B) undesirable …include
C) misleading …ignore
D) adequate …repudiate

8. He is distinguished by _____ that prevents allying himself with _____ movements.

A) a chauvinism … patriotic
B) a clemency… philanthropic
C) an aggressiveness …revolutionary
D) an independence …sectarian

9. Whereas popular music over the past decade consistently _____ creativity and originality, the problem with classical music has been a clear lack of _____.

A) demonstrated … innovation
B) avoided …. development
C) embellished…motivation
D) circumscribed…acceptance

10. The discovery that interstellar _____ exist _____ scientific hypothesis that the expanses between these are devoid of matter.

A) galaxies …. revived
B) constellations …. prompted
C) molecules …demolished
D) vastness …challenged

SENTENCE COMPLETION SET 2

1. This subtle _____ of the senator's character, though crafted by _____ hand, is as damaging as anything that a rival could have written.

   A) denigration…an inimical
   B) assassination…an expert
   C) presentation…an illustrious
   D) analysis ... a friendly

2. Although she was not a very_____ writer, the few works she did produce earned for her the adulation of such diverse groups as the avant-garde poets and the _____ literary critics.

   A) creative…radical
   B) prolific…mainstream
   C) lucid…apolitical
   D) capable ... typical

3. Most people are shameless _____ when it comes to the rich & famous celebrities, _____ curious about how they get their money and how they spend it.

   A) prigs…secretly
   B) critics…endlessly
   C) voyeurs… insatiably
   D) exhibition…blatantly

4. Luard implies that rising state centralization is _____ as well as detestable and, so, nowhere sets out a strategy for _____ it.

   A) unfortunate .... modifying
   B) intriguing… evaluating
   C) offensive…opposing
   D) inevitable… resisting

5. The senator was cautioned by her aides that, despite the fact that a vote for the tax bill seems _____ at the present time, it will be a political_____ in the next election.

   A) advantageous ... boon
   B) expedient ... liability
   C) inopportune…embarrassment
   D) deleterious…drawback

6. The blueprints for the new automobile were _____ at first glance, but the designer had been basically too conservative to _____ previous standards of beauty.

A) striking .... flout
B) impractical…ignore
C) impeccable…dispel
D) influential… assess

7. For those Puritans who believed that _____ obligations were imposed by divine will, the correct course of action was not withdrawal from the world but conscientious _____ of the duties of business.

A) practical…mystification
B) inherent…manipulation
C) secular…discharge
D) earthy… disavowal

8. Despite China's 2,000-year old _____ medicinal plants, there was a period in Chinese history when the art of herbal medicine was almost _____.

A) expertise in ... lost
B) bewilderment over ... thwarted
C) ignorance of…eliminated
D) affection for…encouraged

9. Plants store a _____ of water in their leaves, stems, or understock to provide themselves with a form of _____ that will carry them through the inevitable drought they must suffer in the wild.

A) supply… power
B) hoard… insurance
C) reservoir… accommodation
D) provision… restoration

10. The _____ of modernist architecture _____ the natural human desire to celebrate and decorate, to take delight in ornament.

A) elaborateness ... neglects
B) austerity ... recognizes
C) embellishment ... undermines
D) severity ... opposes

SENTENCE COMPLETION SET 3

1. The remark was only slightly _____, inviting, perhaps, a chuckle, but certainly not a _____.

    A) audible… reward
    B) hostile …shrug
    C) amusing …rebuke
    D) humorous…guffaw ⟵ circled

2. Human beings are much less creatures of instinct than other animals are; nearly all our behavior patterns are _____ rather than _____.

    A) learned ... inherited
    B) predictable ... erratic
    C) routine…diversified ⟵ circled
    D) Innate … acquired

3. Although his outnumbered troops fought bravely, the general felt he had no choice but to _____ defeat and _____ a retreat.

    A) hasten ... suggest
    B) seek.... try
    C) oversee…reject
    D) acknowledge.... order ⟵ circled

4. He never published his writings hastily; he allowed time for the tumult of his imagination to _____ and for the novelties of his _____ to grow familiar.

    A) increase ... discovery
    B) rage… invention
    C) abate … convention
    D) subside … creation ⟵ circled

5. Many philosophers agree that the verbal aggression of profanity in certain radical newspapers is not _____ or childish, but an assault on _____ essential to the revolutionaries' purpose.

    A) belligerent ... fallibility
    B) serious…propriety
    C) infallible … sociability ⟵ circled
    D) trivial ... decorum

6. When a person suddenly loses consciousness, a bystander is not expected to _____ the problem but to attempt to _____ its effects by starting vital functions if they are absent.

A) cure ... precipitate
B) minimize... predict
C) determine... detect
D) diagnose...counter

7. Traditional stories concerning the marvels of the medieval cities and empires of western Sudan were ultimately based on historical fact; thus while the stories _____, they did not actually _____.

A) embroidered ... invent
B) criticized ... comment
C) documented ... evaluate
D) Fabricated ... judge

8. Fuentes' subtly persuasive arguments for continuity in Latino culture _____ readers to recognize that their future cannot be _____ from the way they treat their past.

A) implore ... deciphered
B) condition ...inferred
C) invite ... divorced
D) command ... projected

9. The principle of equality should not imply a leveling down, but should be sensitive to the _____ of human needs and to the _____ means that may be required for their satisfaction.

A) universality ... necessary
B) impudence... bold
C) plurality... diverse
D) inequity ... criminal

10. Abstracting the quantitative aspects of physical phenomena often reveals unsuspected _____ because the quantitative laws turn out to be the same for apparently _____ phenomena.

A) incongruities ... analogous
B) differences ... unfamiliar
C) relationships ... dissimilar
D) harmonies ... abstract

SENTENCE COMPLETION SET 4

1. All he ever wanted was his own way, and his desire now was to make a profit in business, but the profit itself was merely the result of victory; the victory itself was in the _____ of his _____.

   A) achievement ... goal
   B) denial ... rights
   C) existence ... predilection
   D) denouement ...drama

2. In their work, microbiologists contend with living forms so _____ in appearance and habits as to _____ the common bond presumed to ally them.

   A) diverse ... belie
   B) homogeneous ... veil
   C) erratic ... validate
   D) conspicuous ... obscure

3. Aerial photography has been an _____ tool over since the discovery that patterns of light and dark green in the first growth of grain often _____ earthworks and roads buried beneath the fields.

   A) archaeological… reflect
   B) astronomical…reveal
   C) agricultural…sense
   D) architectural…determine

4. In addition to his natural predilection for compromise, what motivated the governor to be so _____ the hostile legislature was his acute awareness of his own personal and political _____.

   A) angry at ... popularity
   B) intolerant of…ambitions
   C) respectful of…flexibility
   D) conciliatory toward…isolation

5. Investigators agree, not only that systematic studies failed to _____ answers to the questions of 'what is schizophrenia', but also that the question itself had been _____ formulated.

   A) clarify ... completely
   B) challenge… weakly
   C) enhance…profitably
   D) yield ... incorrectly

6. The practice of _____ coins that end up on edge in flipping experiments illustrates one method of the ambiguous case within a _____ system.

A) ignoring ... classification
B) destroying ... production
C) minting... logical
D) cleaning... scientific

7. Let us remember that _____ is a very dangerous method that permits us to do by degrees that which we would all _____ doing at once.

A) anger ... balk at
B) gradualism ... shrink from
C) apathy ... profit from
D) fanaticism... prefer

8. Our initial comprehension of the assumptions by which people act, or say they act, is _____ by a growing sense of the _____ between professed and genuine beliefs.

A) reconsidered ... correlation
B) disrupted ... parallelism
C) confirmed... discrepancy
D) modified ... dissonance

9. Although they are _____ by traps, poison, and shotguns, predators _____ to feast on flocks of sheep.

A) lured ... refuse
B) destroyed... cease
C) impeded ...continue
D) encouraged ... attempt

10. Our highly _____ vocabulary for street crime compared with our _____ vocabulary for corporate crime corresponds to the general public's unawareness extent of corporate crime.

A) nuanced ... subtle
B) uninformative ... misleading
C) euphemistic ... abstract
D) differentiated ... limited

SENTENCE COMPLETION SET 5

1. Just as it is illogical to denounce a museum for its paintings, it is quite uncommon, even for those unenthusiastic about sports, to criticize _____ for outcomes of _____.

   A) team… coach
   B) stadiums… matches *(circled)*
   C) athletes…snobbery
   D) scholars… apathy

2. Because the order in which the parts of speech appear in the sentences of a given language is decided merely by custom, it is _____ to maintain that every departure from that order constitutes a _____ of a natural law.

   A) traditional… transformation
   B) conventional…transgression
   C) necessary ... prototype
   D) unjustifiable…violation

3. Ultimately, the book's credibility is strained, the slender, though far from _____, web of evidence presented on one salient point is expected to support a vast _____ of implications.

   A) unconvincing…cacophony
   B) nonexistent…superstructure
   C) indispensable…array
   D) intricate…network

4. One reason why pertinent fossils are _____ is that crucial stages of evolution occurred in the tropics where it is difficult to explore for fossils, and so their discovery has _____.

   A) unique .... resulted
   B) unconcealable .... declined
   C) uncommon .... lagged *(circled)*
   D) recent .... resumed

5. It is an error to regard the imagination as a mainly _____ force; if it destroys and alters, it also _____ hitherto isolated beliefs, insights, and mental habits into strongly unified systems.

   A) visionary…conjures
   B) beneficial… converts
   C) revolutionary ... fuses
   D) negative…shunts *(circled)*

6. Every novel invites us to enter a world that is initially strange; our gradual and selective orientation to its manners _____ infants' _____ to their environment.

A) imitates…welcome
B) completes… introduction
C) resembles… adjustment
D) alters... blindness

7. As the creation of new knowledge through science has become _____, resistance to innovation has become less _____, taking the form of inertia rather than direct attack.

A) controversial ... sporadic
B) institutionalized ... aggressive
C) essential ... effective
D) public… circumspect

8. Rousseau's short discourse, a work that was generally _____ the cautious, unadorned prose of the day, deviated from that prose style in its _____ discussion of the physical sciences.

A) critical of ... lengthy
B) superior to ... austere
C) bolder than … intelligent
D) consistent with ... unrestrained

9. A truly _____ historian of science, Meyer neither _____ the abilities of the scientists she presents nor condescends to them.

A) unbiased…scrutinizes
B) objective…inflates
C) impressionable ... patronizes
D) reverent…admires

10. The losing animal in a struggle saves itself from destruction by an act of _____, an act usually recognized and _____ by the winner.

A) submission ... accepted
B) hostility…avoided
C) bluffing… reaffirmed
D) anger… condoned

SENTENCE COMPLETION SET 6

1. Social democracy has thrived in 21st century Western Europe because it improves the living standards of the _____ while keeping the fears of the upper classes _____.

   A) journalists...satisfied
   B) proletariat...allayed
   C) plutocrats...stymied
   D) bards...stoked

2. The tactics of dictators all over the world are similar - _____ the people and slap _____ charges against those who protest.

   A) encourage...cancellation
   B) subjugate...sedition
   C) condition...demolition
   D) bamboozle...attention

3. The new substitute teacher was a _____ in classroom management and was not able to handle a class full of _____ children.

   A) maestro...somnolent
   B) novice...beatific
   C) tyro...rambunctious
   D) grinch...raucous

4. When Indiana Jones attempted to remove the Mayan _____ from the underground temple, a trap sprung and a thick _____ fluid started dripping from a hole in the ceiling.

   A) pyramid...ambitious
   B) relic...viscous
   C) tomb...crystalline
   D) artifact...cantankerous

5. The army's treatment of the enemy prisoners of war is _____ and is bound to invite _____ on our own soldiers captured by the enemy.

   A) encouraging...revenge
   B) consoling...happiness
   C) appalling...retribution
   D) expensive...annihilation

6. I couldn't believe that the _____ little lady who looked like my grandmother was an _____ fan of death metal music.

A) murderous...mediocre
B) wizened…meticulous
C) monumental...ardent
D) mousy...avid

7. We do not have any information about the mysterious _____ afflicting princess Margaret as the palace officials are very _____ about the whole affair.

A) malady...cagey
B) relationship...forthcoming
C) gentleman...apologetic
D) scheme...callous

8. The second colony succeeded in gaining a foothold in the hostile environment because the _____ colonists were fortunate to have the _____ Mr. Gomez as an adviser.

A) plucky...sagacious
B) ignorant...atrocious
C) nubile...nonchalant
D) lucky...incompetent

9. Ms. Mulvaney was enjoying a _____ afternoon at the office, when her peace was disturbed by _____ man demanding to see the manager.

A) serene...a momentous
B) busy...a decrepit
C) simmering...an unremarkable
D) tranquil...an officious

10. The new classical edition of *Gilgamesh* that _____ all the previous versions, manages the difficult task of being comprehensive without becoming _____.

A) surrenders...complicated
B) survives...copious
C) supersedes...pedantic
D) encompasses...spoiled

SENTENCE COMPLETION SET 7

1. The political polarization of America has reached the world of search engines with Google being accused of _____ search results throwing up pages with _____ views on Key Topics.

   A) filtering...rotational
   B) censoring...conservative
   C) encouraging...abrasive
   D) commiserating...aggressive

2. The 2020 attack on the Kabul general hospital was so horrific that even groups that sought _____ for terrorists like Bin Laden are refusing to defend the _____ who carried it out.

   A) amnesty...fanatics
   B) clemency...adulterers
   C) credibility...murderers
   D) parole...autocrats

3. The global effort to _____ malaria has stalled due to the emergence of new strains of *Plasmodium* that are _____ to standard anti-malarial drug cocktails.

   A) eradicate...impervious
   B) cultivate...resistant
   C) eliminate...susceptible
   D) aggravate...welcoming

4. The _____ new curriculum is not challenging enough for the students and is proving to be a _____ to rapidly improve learning outcomes.

   A) interesting...precedence
   B) mediocre...mole hill
   C) burnished...panacea
   D) vapid...hindrance

5. The health care workers surveying the pandemic infected neighborhoods have become _____ to the _____ hurled at them by the disgruntled members of the public.

   A) busy...projectiles
   B) adept...clichés
   C) blasé..invectives
   D) immune...accolades

6. The funeral was a moving affair with the dead woman's seven year old niece singing the traditional _____ with her _____ voice.

A) dirge...rapacious
B) attire...melodious
C) elegy...mellifluous
D) canard...piquant

7. Engels doesn't spare the French radicals either - his book is full of _____ criticism toward their _____ attitudes.

A) sloppy...loquacious
B) withering...libertine
C) subtle...breathtaking
D) viscous...lackadaisical

8. Though Gandhi's *My Experiments With Truth* _____ endorses veganism, it _____ from calling for a blanket ban on meat and other animal products.

A) vigorously...strays
B) implicitly...abstains
C) religiously...grates
D) reluctantly...belies

9. The federal government's _____ on the states' traditional rights to frame their own healthcare policy has had a _____ effect on their ability to deal with the pandemic.

A) adorning...brutal
B) rubbishing...spectacular
C) endorsement...salubrious
D) impingement...debilitating

10. It is a little bit _____ to see how the children from the refugee camps have become _____ at sleeping through an artillery barrage.

A) disconcerting...adept
B) disheartening...mollycoddled
C) regulating...experts
D) anointing...proficient

SENTENCE COMPLETION SET 8

1. Germany's _____ claim that its invasion of the Soviet Union was _____ in nature did not fool any of its nominal allies let alone the neutral nations.

   A) mendacious...preemptive
   B) audacious...toxic
   C) fallacious...pertinent
   D) gargantuan...impartial

2. A country whose economy is propped by the billions of dollars in _____ from its citizens working in foreign countries adopting a protectionist trade policy is _____ to say the least.

   A) remittances...oxymoronic
   B) fines...thoughtful
   C) balances...karmic
   D) transfers...consoling

3. China is fast emerging as the most _____ nation in Asia and has supplanted Russia as the primary _____ of the United States.

   A) arrogant...comrade
   B) altruistic...placebo
   C) ambitious...spectrum
   D) puissant...adversary

4. The _____ old woman had to come out of her semi-retirement to urge the factions to _____ their petty differences and work together.

   A) juvenile...ignore
   B) doddering...aggravate
   C) callow...bury
   D) wizened...transcend

5. Though belief in spirits is suspected to be _____ amongst immigrants from some countries, it is difficult to get hard numbers on the practice as the community members are quick to shut down any discussion on the topic as _____.

   A) abhorrent ...stylish
   B) pervasive...blasphemous
   C) prevalent...hedonistic
   D) heretical...banal

6. The _____ policies of the Food and Drug Administration agency have backfired and led to _____ drugs from third world countries flooding the market.

A) astute….ambitious
B) half-baked...adulterated
C) acute....automated
D) atrocious...ambivalent

7. The nobleman chosen by the old king to become his daughter's _____ turned out to be a _____ of the highest order.

A) confidant...chaplain
B) partisan...idiot
C) consort...charlatan
D) adviser...caricature

8. All the warnings of the counter-intelligence experts about the _____ region famous for medical tourism being targeted by insurgents have so far elicited only _____ reaction from the governor.

A) diffused...an ambitious
B) anachronistic...a muted
C) salubrious...an anodyne
D) seditious...a notarized

9. Despite having a wide _____ of courses to choose from for her undergraduate degree, Monique chose to study a mathematics course with statistics as _____ subject.

A) spectrum...an ancillary
B) cornucopia...an addendum
C) range...a curve
D) difference...a node

10. Many political scientists believe that the Governor's _____ activities have _____ the institution of governorship like no other scandal before.

A) noxious...uplifted
B) amorous...abased
C) unethical...encouraged
D) sinister...supplanted

SENTENCE COMPLETION SET 9

1. The unapologetic way in which _____ like Richard Dawkins go about criticizing religious dogma has been denounced by believers as _____ and unwarranted.

   A) parsons...beatific
   B) atheists...boorish
   C) bourgeoisie....bellicose
   D) strumpets...benign

2. After the botched _____ of the nationwide Medical Program led to a small increase in insurance premiums, the _____ for rolling back the program became louder.

   A) adjournment...expectation
   B) implementation...clamor
   C) elimination...demand
   D) evolution...fatigue

3. Even trace amounts of lead in water pipes has been proven to have _____ effects on children and causes ailments that require expensive treatment and prolonged _____.

   A) divergent...confrontation
   B) timorous...medication
   C) statutory...relapse
   D) deleterious...convalescence

4. While the firemen were _____ about using a firefighting helicopter over a densely populated urban area, the fire _____ out of control.

   A) dithering...billowed
   B) hesitating...overflowed
   C) demonstrating...surged
   D) calculating...quenched

5. Any _____ that the board felt when they heard about the next quarter's projected profits quickly disappeared when the CEO added the _____ that the projections were highly speculative.

   A) tendency...qualification
   B) confusion...source
   C) elation...caveat
   D) relief...canard

6. It is impossible to _____ the exact number of casualties in the war because both sides only publish highly _____ accounts.

A) conjure….speculative
B) ascertain...embellished
C) collate...emotional
D) abridge...censored

7. If the mayor wants to preserve the _____ between the communities, he has to stop _____ and speak bluntly.

A) animosity...calculating
B) amity...equivocating
C) integrity...hiccupping
D) antecedents...desecrating

8. The department of motor vehicles is _____ by decades of following unimaginative procedures and is _____ about not adopting new software that would make their processes more efficient.

A) hidebound...adamant
B) hobbled...virulent
C) enabled...aroused
D) shackled...analogous

9. The sudden _____ of the Denarius by emperor Justinian showed the Greek traders how _____ they were to use the Roman currency as a standard of exchange.

A) cladding...ignoble
B) encirclement...fallible
C) enlargement...visionary
D) debasement...gullible

10. The Allied strategists were not able to _____ the target of the U-Boat wolf pack because all the enemy radio intercepts were heavily _____.

A) discover...dramatic
B) discern...garbled
C) destroy...animated
D) differentiate...corrosive

SENTENCE COMPLETION SET 10

1. To _____ his guilt about using illegal means to become rich, Adams started spending his huge fortune for the _____ of the poor.

   A) amortize...liberation
   B) absolve...alienation
   C) assuage...emancipation
   D) alleviate...incarceration

2. The CDC is usually _____ when it comes to providing sensitive data about disease outbreaks but this time it has been _____ sharing its projections and models with epidemiologists across the world.

   A) eager...gladly
   B) circumspect...liberally
   C) cagey...hilariously
   D) resolved...easily

3. Despite making obvious attempts to _____ ethnic minority groups within its borders, the Dictator insists that its actions do not _____ the Geneva Conventions.

   A) annihilate...contravene
   B) cleanse...condone
   C) eliminate...contraband
   D) emancipate...embrace

4. Small towns that are not _____ about maintaining a budget surplus when the economy is doing good _____ go bankrupt during times of recession.

   A) careless...confusingly
   B) proactive...capriciously
   C) calculative...unexpectedly
   D) conscientious...invariably

5. The 1960s, known as the decade of discontent, saw people from _____ backgrounds leave their comfortable lives behind and become followers of godmen in an attempt to attain _____ .

   A) rural...statehood
   B) disparate...nirvana
   C) homogeneous...liberation
   D) lugubrious...enlightenment

6. As the _____ reports of defeat poured in from various states, a _____ silence descended over the campaign headquarters.

A) advantageous...miserable
B) uncontrolled...miserly
C) inevitable...melancholy
D) detailed...blithe

7. The _____ toward the use of poison gas in the battlefield ended with World War I and none of the countries use it _____ anymore.

A) preference...clandestinely
B) predisposition...overtly
C) composition...dependably
D) revulsion...animatedly

8. _____ of women's rights have started maintaining a _____ of laws they say are effectively penalizing women for just being women.

A) negotiators....storage
B) opponents...silo
C) advocates...compendium
D) meddlers...library

9. The documents submitted for the expert committee's _____ clearly established that the lunch served in the district's schools was _____ in nutrients.

A) perusal...deficient
B) entertainment...munificent
C) edification...magnificent
D) allocation...mired

10. The New England Patriots are known for their _____ and their uncharacteristically subdued play yesterday must be _____.

A) pugnacity...an aberration
B) arrogance...a distraction
C) skill...an examination
D) unpredictability...a gratification

SENTENCE COMPLETION SET 11

1. The old curator was _____ to hear that the mob had broken into the museum and _____ its collection of antiques.

   A) crestfallen...desecrated
   B) overjoyed...ruptured
   C) copious...plundered
   D) penitent...pillaged

2. The horrors cooked up by Stephen King's _____ imagination have kept three successive generations of readers _____ in his books.

   A) conniving...captive
   B) infantile...abrogated
   C) moribund...mired
   D) fecund...engrossed

3. Any trade concession given by the neighboring country under _____ always _____ bilateral relations in the long term as the neighbor does not forget the insult.

   A) compulsion...reviews
   B) blackmail...encourages
   C) duress...hampers
   D) sanction...bullies

4. The _____ with which the border guards are mistreating the _____ at the checkpoint is the direct consequence of the xenophobia ginned up by the government.

   A) tendency...dancers
   B) compassion...athletes
   C) impunity...immigrants
   D) jocularity...tourists

5. The loss of _____ caused by the public meltdown of the senator proved _____ and he was defeated in the primary.

   A) support....replaceable
   B) esteem...irremediable
   C) passion...lovable
   D) momentum...agreeable

6. The Olympic athlete had a _____ young body, long red hair, and big green eyes and was described by a commentator as _____-like.

   A) creepy...man
   B) wizened...ape
   C) doddering...troll
   D) lithe...nymph

7. Nearly two hundred years after the end of the Crimean war, a new book has come out claiming to have _____ proof that the war was precipitated by the _____ behavior of the Russian ambassador at a feast organized by the Ottoman Sultan.

   A) speculative...serene
   B) incontrovertible...gluttonous
   C) captive....abominable
   D) fresh...absent

8. The nationalistic _____ put out by the jingoistic media proved to be extremely _____ to maintaining cordial relations with the neighboring countries.

   A) hyperbole...inimical
   B) propaganda...cheerful
   C) announcements...horrendous
   D) pamphlets...alarming

9. No amount of apologies or reparations would _____ the memory of the great _____ - a mass movement of six million African Americans out of the Southern United States in the early 20th century.

   A) exorcise...migration
   B) expunge...merriment
   C) honor...befuddlement
   D) canoodle...depression

10. The main challenge before Geitner's economic team was to _____ a bailout plan that would penalize the lawbreakers while keeping the existing financial framework _____.

    A) formulate...intact
    B) devise...triumphant
    C) gaslight...chugging
    D) synergize...terrified

SENTENCE COMPLETION SET 12

1. The cab stopped before a _____ looking building guarded by two machine gun toting guards who stared _____ at the passersby.

   A) debris...balefully
   B) seedy...malevolently
   C) facile...happily
   D) grumpy...dazedly

2. The income inequality in the post-cold war era is _____ by the excesses of the American _____ with the protection of the law.

   A) accentuated...plutocrats
   B) proscribed...lawmakers
   C) underscored...crackpots
   D) absolved...billionaires

3. Every morning Cage woke up to the drill sergeant _____ "Good morning boys! Battle is the Great Redeemer. It is the fiery _____ in which true heroes are forged!"

   A) bellowing...crucible
   B) cooing...cookpot
   C) bluffing...cauldron
   D) whispering...freezer

4. The interior of the salon looked like the aftermath of a natural _____ - broken glass and other _____ were strewn everywhere.

   A) disaster...accountants
   B) medication...utensils
   C) calamity...debris
   D) tendency...pieces

5. The Diaspora Museum in Tel Aviv has painstakingly _____ several artifacts from around the world that remind the visitors about the _____ contributions of the Jewish people.

   A) recreated....informal
   B) collected...wholesome
   C) prescribed...heinous
   D) compiled... multifarious

6. Florence Nightingale, the _____ nurse considered as a pioneer of the modern hospital system, was _____ at the callous attitude of the British administrators toward famine victims.

A) visible...upset
B) vibrant...terrified
C) visionary...aghast
D) villainous...irate

7. The lab director has _____ that the cuts to the university's budget have _____ his employees to ignore safety procedures.

A) alleged...compelled
B) announced...educated
C) confessed...lubricate
D) pleaded...empowered

8. After Frederick the Great _____ the Prussian army and equipped it with modern weapons, it easily _____ the minor rebellions of the Junkers.

A) encouraged...skilled
B) revamped...quelled
C) constituted...leveraged
D) renovated...quenched

9. The _____ way in which the police handled the investigation has _____ a golden opportunity to get rid of the city's drug lords.

A) amateurish...squandered
B) appealing...squashed
C) appalling...relieved
D) atrocious...elevated

10. The papal bill of 1493 resolved the longstanding _____ between Portugal and Spain over sharing the _____ of the New World.

A) drama...borders
B) dispute...bounty
C) treaty...sins
D) tension...acclaim

Sentence Completion (1 Blank) Answers

SET 1		SET 2		SET 3		SET 4		SET 5	
Q No.	Answer	Q No.	Answer	Q No.	Answer	Q No.	Answer	Q No.	Answer
1	D	1	C	1	A	1	B	1	C
2	D	2	D	2	D	2	C	2	C
3	A	3	B	3	D	3	B	3	C
4	B	4	A	4	D	4	D	4	D
5	B	5	B	5	A	5	B	5	A
6	A	6	C	6	D	6	A	6	B
7	D	7	C	7	B	7	A	7	B
8	B	8	D	8	B	8	A	8	C
9	D	9	A	9	C	9	C	9	D
10	D	10	A	10	B	10	A	10	A

SET 6		SET 7		SET 8		SET 9		SET 10	
Q No.	Answer	Q No.	Answer	Q No.	Answer	Q No.	Answer	Q No.	Answer
1	D	1	B	1	D	1	D	1	A
2	B	2	B	2	C	2	C	2	B
3	C	3	C	3	B	3	B	3	A
4	D	4	D	4	A	4	A	4	D
5	A	5	A	5	D	5	D	5	C
6	A	6	B	6	A	6	C	6	B
7	B	7	D	7	B	7	B	7	A
8	C	8	A	8	C	8	A	8	D
9	D	9	B	9	D	9	D	9	C
10	D	10	C	10	A	10	C	10	B

SET 11		SET 12	
Q No.	Answer	Q No.	Answer
1	A	1	C
2	B	2	D
3	C	3	A
4	D	4	B
5	A	5	C
6	B	6	C
7	C	7	D
8	D	8	A
9	A	9	D
10	B	10	A

Detailed Explanations (1Blank) Set 1-5

EXPLANATIONS SET 1 (1 BLANK)

1. (D) The word *ironic* signifies a contradiction of ideas within the sentence, and the conjunction *while* indicates that the characteristics of the *good* and *evil* people are being contrasted. Therefore, if the good people are often dull, the evil people must be having a characteristic which is the opposite of being dull. Among the given choices, it is only the word *fascinating* that has such a meaning, and is the answer.

2. (D) The phrase "must be at least modified, *if not* ... " indicates that the missing word must mean an action which is somewhat stronger than *modified*. Among the given choices, it is only *overturned* which has such a meaning

3. (A) How can you describe the fact that a person, who grew up in a region *rich in American Indian culture,* did *not* develop her interest in Native American art *until adulthood,* but *later wrote* a *very sensitive and authoritative book on it?* Not as *satisfactory,* or *doubtful,* or *concerned.* The only appropriate word among the given choices is *ironic.*

4. (B) The use of the conjunction *although* implies a contrast within the sentence. The first part of the sentence talks of two types of states, namely *maturational* and *developmental,* and says that they occur in an *orderly sequence.* So, one should normally expect that their timings, with regard to their *onsets* (meaning *commencement)* and *durations,* must be *equal* or *similar.* But, because of the use of the conjunction *although,* we should infer that the author wishes to say *exactly the opposite,* namely, that their timings, with regard to *onset* and *duration,* are *not equal or similar.* Among the choices, *varies* is the only word which has this meaning, and is the answer.

5. (B) The use of the conjunction *although* indicates *an implied contrast* within the sentence. The latter part of the sentence says that, when *tempered with other elements,* the substance referred to could be *stored safely in metal containers.* So, the first part should mean that the *normal property* of the substance is *to corrode* metal containers. Among the choices, it is only the word *caustic* that has this meaning, and is the answer.

6. (A) The clue lies in the phrase 'like a character who has *stumbled on stage by mistake'.* The missing adjective must therefore be descriptive of something which is present at a place *by mistake. Anomalous* (meaning *abnormal, irregular)* is the only word among the choices having this meaning, and is the answer. You might have been tempted to choose *derelict* as the answer. But this word means 'deserted', 'neglected' or 'forsaken', and does not fit logically in the given sentence.

7. (D) We can surmise from the sentence that Maroon societies are African groups. The

sentence says that their culture has not remained *static* at the seventeenth-century level, but *has been adapted creatively to their changing lives.* The missing verb must therefore be a *synonym* of this italicized phrase. Among the choices it is *modified* which has a similar meaning, and is the answer.

8. (B) If the criticism by Thackeray of Dickens' novel *Oliver Twist* was based on the former's view that the *cult* (meaning the *glorification*) *of the criminal* was dangerous, we can surmise that, in this novel, Dickens must have depicted some criminals as *attractive* or *heroic* characters. Among the choices, *threatening, conniving* (meaning *scheming*), *fearsome* and *irritating* do not make the criminals such *attractive* characters. So, you must choose *riveting* as the only possible answer, even if you do not know its meaning. In fact, *riveting* means *attracting/compelling,* and fits in well in this sentence.

9. (D) The second part of the sentence says that anyone who reads the ambassador's papers *slowly* and *attentively* will be *richly repaid.* The fact that one should read the papers *slowly* and *attentively* for getting the full benefit from them implies that what is contained in them is *difficult material.* Among the choices, 'The ambassador's papers are *not easy reading'* is what brings out this meaning clearly, and is the answer. If his papers are not *valuable* or *insightful* reading, then none can be *richly repaid* by reading them. So, (B) and (C) are wrong. The phrase *'petty* reading' is not appropriate for an *ambassador's* papers.

10. (D) The key to the correct choice is in the word *though,* which indicates that the missing word must convey a sense which is the *opposite* of the phrase 'having certain characteristics in common'. Among the choices, *diverse* (meaning *various* or *differing in qualities),* is the most suitable answer. The sentence now means that though people ask *diverse* questions, there are *some common characteristics* among them.

EXPLANATIONS SET 2 (1 BLANK)

1. (C) The use of the phrase *'divulging* his *frank* opinions' implies that the employee *did not agree* with the proposals of the company. But, if he felt *intimidated,* what would he do with these opinions? He would either *keep them to himself* or *merely hint at them,* being *afraid of expressing them openly. Chary of* (meaning *being cautious about)* is the phrase which conveys this meaning, and is the answer.

2. (D) If we are being *forced* to *surrender* to the *authority* of the clock, then systematic timekeeping cannot be said to be imposing a form of *anarchy* or *permanence* or *provincialism* or *autonomy* on us. The three italicized words in the first part of the sentence above indicate that it is imposing a form of *tyranny* on us. So, (D) is the answer.

3. (B) This question is best answered by inserting each of the choices in the given blank, and testing which of them lends a cogent meaning to the sentence. The core part of the given sentence is, *"After the war,* the consumer demand ___ *defense effort* as a *stimulus to industry".* Since defense effort could not have been *included* as a stimulus to industry *after the war,* (A) is wrong. "After the war, the consumer demand *replaced* the defense effort as a stimulus to industry" is an eminently logical statement, because industrial activity *during the war* would have been *geared to the demands* of the *defense* effort, and such activity would have been *scaled down* after the war was over, necessitating a *different type of demand* to stimulate the industry. So, (B) is the answer. The phrases "consumer demand *released* the defense effort", "consumer demand *aroused* the defense effort" and "consumer demand *satisfied* the defense effort" do not make logical sense.

4. (A) What the sentence says is that an infant's *reactions* to its *first stressful experiences* are part of a natural process of development and are not *"harbingers* (meaning *forerunners* or *indicators)* of *childhood unhappiness* or of *adolescent anxiety".* The parallel structure employed by the author in this sentence indicates that the missing word must have meaning similar to *harbingers.* Among the choices, *prophetic* is the only word with such a meaning, and is the answer.

5. (B) Though this is a long and involved sentence, the clue phrase to the correct answer ('sense of *uniqueness* of the central concept') is available in the first line itself. Which adjective is most suitable to describe a mode of study that is needed to unravel a *unique* central concept? Among the choices, it is *distinctive* that is most appropriate. (On the other hand, *all* subjects will require a *thorough, dependable* and *scientific* mode of study, while the phrase *'dynamic* mode of study' does not make any sense.)

6. (C) Something which is *needed* for life, even if it is in extremely small quantities, cannot be described as *destructive* to life, or *insignificant* to life, or *extraneous* to life, or *vulnerable* to life. It can only be described as being *essential* to life. So, (C) is the answer

7. (C) The use of the conjunction *whereas* indicates that the first part of the sentence is

contrasted with the second part. The first part implies that, before the 1930's, knowledge had the *quality of permanence*. So, the second part must mean that today's knowledge, particularly that relating to scientific developments, *tends to become outdated soon.* Among the given choices, it is only the word *obsolete* that has this meaning, and is the answer.

8. (D) The use of the conjunction 'but' implies the existence of a *contradiction* within the sentence. *Monomania* means *'obsession, to the point of madness, with* a *single task or subject',* and is usually not considered as a desirable quality in any person. But the use of the conjunction *but* implies that the author of the sentence does *not* consider Murray's monomania as *harmful.* So the missing word must have a *positive* connotation. We can therefore eliminate the choices *tame* (meaning *cowardly), tendentious* (meaning *dishonest)* and *meretricious* (meaning *gaudy).* The phrase, "his monomania must be regarded as a *beneficent* or *at least an innocuous* one" makes eminent sense. So, (D) is the answer.

9. (A) The question can be answered by fitting the four answer choices in the blank and see which one makes sense. (A) makes the most sense as the sentence talks about the problems created by cutting down of trees - *generate* is the only choice that is synonymous with *create*.

10. (A) What are the things that go through a complex network of *producers* and *consumers?* Not *dividends,* nor *communications,* nor *nutrients. Commodities* is the only suitable word among the choices, and is the answer.

EXPLANATIONS SET 3 (1 BLANK)

1. (A) The committee mentioned in the sentence has obviously studied some specific problems, and has offered suggestions to solve them. If the committee has also *warned* that the non-implementation of these suggestions would *eventually* render the problems *insoluble,* it means that, according to it, these problems would *become worse* with the passage of time. Among the choices, *exacerbated* is the only word which has this meaning, and is the answer. *(Insurmountable* and *insoluble* have the same meaning; therefore, it is not logical to say that *'insurmountable* problems would *eventually* become *insoluble'.* So, (B) is *not* the appropriate choice.)

2. (D) What will the ability of carbon atom to form *an unending* series *of different molecules* result in? Among the given choices, *variety* is the only suitable word which can describe this result, and is the answer.

3. (D) Apparently, the author of the sentence and his friends were under the impression that the woman was *supporting* their new program. So, when she *refused* a *make* a *speech* in its favor, what would they have newly learnt about her support to the program? Obviously that such support was *only half-hearted.* The phrase, "It was *less than whole-hearted"* expresses just this, and is the answer.

4. (D) The phrase "Carlos Saura is *not given to explicit statement"* means that, in his movies, he tries to communicate his messages to the audience through *indirect references* (as a result of which those who cannot understand such indirect references are left *puzzled and unmoved).* Among the choices, it is *allusiveness* (meaning *indirect references)* which has this meaning, is the answer.

5. (A) The phrase *'although* their *pronunciations* have *changed'* indicates an *implied contrast* between the two parts of the sentence. This means that the *spellings* of the words (referred to in the first part) must have *remained unchanged* over a period of time only word among the choices which means *unchanged* is *preserved,* which is the answer.

6. (D) The use of the conjunction *although* implies that there is a *contradiction in sense* within the sentence. The second part says that fear and aggression are *distinct* (meaning *different),* both *physiologically* and *psychologically.* In order to bring out the implied contrast, the missing word must describe a state in which these two are *quite similar* or *lack distinctiveness.* The only possible words among the choices are *simultaneous* and *transitional.* Between the two, the word *simultaneous* must be ruled out because, in that case, the phrase must read 'simultaneous states *of* fear and aggression', and 'not simultaneous states *between* fear and aggression'. The word *transitional* refers to a stage of movement from one state to another *when the qualities of both states are present together* and the difference between them is *blurred.* It is this word which fits in logically in the given sentence, and is the answer.

7. (B) *(Cant* means *affectedly solemn; arcane* means *mysterious; uninitiated listener* refers to a person *who has not been taught the intricacies of music appreciation.)* A process that is *closed to the uninitiated listener* cannot be appropriately described as *unreliable,* or as *arrogant,* or as *elementary.* If a process is *intuitive,* no one need *initiate* a listener to it. So, choices (A), (C), and (D) are all inappropriate. An *arcane* (meaning *mysterious)* process may require a person to be *initiated* to it before he can understand it. So, (B) completes a meaningful sentence, and is the answer.

8. (B) *Renewable* resources are those that can be grown again and again, like timber. Timber can also be *preserved* in large quantities *(stockpiled)* for use by future generations. Though wild-life can be *multiplied* by suitable conservation measures, they cannot be *stockpiled,* since wild-life, just as human beings, will *also die periodically.* So, (B) is the answer. You can easily see that none of the other choices fits in with the meaning of the sentence.

9. (C) (A 'Take home examination' means an examination in which the question paper is allowed to be taken home by a student for being answered by himself, and then submitted to his teacher for valuation). The sentence seeks to *contrast* the attitudes of two sets of students - those who interpret the honor code *strictly,* and those who do not consider it wrong to answer the take-home examinations on behalf of other less intelligent students. Obviously, those students who interpret the honor code *strictly* would hold that no student should attempt to answer the take-home examination on behalf of another student. They would, therefore, not consider the practice of a brighter student answering the home examination of a less bright student as *remedial,* or *irreproachable,* or *irrelevant.* They would certainly consider this practice as *unconscionable* (meaning *against one's conscience* or *immoral).* So, (C) is the answer.

10. (B) The use of the phrase *that is* immediately after the blank implies that it is the missing word that has been elaborated as "not using strong language, nor tackling a controversial issue". Among the given choices, it is only *innocuous* (meaning *harmless)* that has this meaning, and is the answer.

EXPLANATIONS SET 4 (1 BLANK)

1. (B) This is a rather long and involved sentence, and the correct answer can be got by inserting each of the answer choices in the blank, and testing *which of the resulting sentences makes logical sense.* If scientists have a considerable *interest* in the possibility that increasing levels of atmospheric carbon-dioxide can cause *long-term* warming effects, it is *illogical* to say that such interest will be sustained *only until* the *current warming trend exceeds the range of normal climatic fluctuations.* In fact, scientific interest in the phenomenon should be logically expected to *increase* if the current warming trend *exceeds* the range of *normal* climatic fluctuations. So, (A) is wrong. Since *long-term warming trends* caused by increasing levels of carbon dioxide are *detrimental to life on earth,* scientists cannot be having an *enthusiasm* for such a possibility. So, (C) is wrong. While scientists would certainly *worry about* the trend, such worry cannot be only *upto the period* until the current warming trend exceeds the range of normal climatic fluctuations. So, (D) is also wrong. (B) implies that climatic fluctuations are quite normal, and some scientists will not consider the current warming trend to be solely attributable to the increasing levels of atmospheric carbon-dioxide, until the warming trend exceeds the range of normal climatic fluctuations. In other words, as at present, they are *uncertain* about the possibility that the current warming trend does not have a normal character but *is attributable to atmospheric carbon-dioxide which may even cause long-term warming effects.* So, (B) is the answer.

2. (C) The phrase *"whatever* its transcendental claims" implies that there is a *contradiction* within the sentence. The sentence now implies that there is a difference between the *theory* (or *transcendental claims)* of politics and what the missing word stands for. So, the missing word cannot also be *theory,* and (A) is wrong. *'Systematic organization* of common *hatreds"* cannot be considered to be the *ideal* of politics. So, (B) is wrong. The statement, "Politics *as a practice,* whatever its *theory* may claim, has always been the systematic organization of common hatreds" forms a meaningful sentence, and brings out the intended contrast sharply. So, (C) is the answer. Though the phrase 'politics as a contest' is by itself acceptable, it does not bring out the *contrast* with the phrase 'whatever its *transcendental claims',* and is not a better choice than (C). So, (D) is wrong.

3. (B) If the *clan system* serves as a method of *checks and balances,* the natural result will be that any One Clan *cannot* assume authoritarian rule over *all* the others. So, the obvious role of the clan system is to *prevent* the emergence of such an authoritarian rule. So, (B) is the answer.

4. (D) This sentence obviously describes a particular woman both in *her capacity as a politician* (woman mayor) and in *her capacity as an individual* (private person), and asserts that the mayor was 'no more and no less' than the private person that she was. In

other words, one *could not distinguish* between her two personalities, that *there was no hypocrisy in her,* and the *one* exactly represented the *other.* Among the choices, it is the word *indivisible* which has this meaning, and is the answer.

5. (B) The use of the conjunction *because* shows that the first part of the sentence must be *a logical and consequent result* of what is stated in the second part. The missing adjective in the sentence must therefore describe a person who *consistently shows distrust of human nature and human motives. Cynical* is the exact word which describes such a person, and is the answer.

6. (A) The person referred to in the sentence is an *unbeliever,* and does *not* have faith in the mysteries of religion. If he had been *small-minded,* he would have *criticized* or *denounced* these mysteries, thus hurting the feelings of the *believers.* But, if he had been *broad-minded,* he would have kept his skepticism *to himself,* and *not openly criticized* or *denounced* the mysteries of religion. So, (A) is the answer. You can see that none of the other choices is consistent with the description of the person as *broadminded.*

7. (A) (The use of the conjunction "but" indicates the existence of a *contrast* within the sentence.) The latter part of the sentence says that dreams, *when they are combined with other data* can *tell us much* about the dreamer. In order to bring out the intended contrast, the earlier part must mean that dreams *by themselves cannot tell us anything about the dreamer.* Among the choices, it is the word *uninformative* that has this meaning, and is the answer.

8. (A) *(Cosmos* means *universe)* The use of the conjunction *because* implies that the second part of the sentence must be *a logical consequence* of the first part. The first part says that modern scientists find the ancient view of the universe *outdated* and *irrelevant.* If so, what will be the nature of their interest in such an *outdated* and *irrelevant* view? Certainly not *intrinsic* or *astronomical* or *experimental* (because astronomical theories, unlike theories of physics or chemistry, are not based on *experiment,* but are based on *observation).* "That the modern scientists consider the outdated Greek theory as of *only historical interest"* completes a cogent sentence. So, (A) is the answer.

9. (C) If Joan's job allowed her *no relaxation,* and posed the *challenge* of dealing with a variety of problems day after day, it could not have resulted in *leisure, monotony, privacy* or *inertia* for her. It could only have resulted in *pressure* on her time and mind. So, (C) is the answer.

10. (A) The first part of the sentence means that, in folk art, *intense feeling* of the artist *takes precedence* over *technical mastery.* This will obviously make it *easier* for the artist to communicate his emotion to the viewer *directly.* Among the given choices, it is *facilitates* that has this meaning, and is the answer.

EXPLANATIONS SET 5 (1 BLANK)

1. (C) The blank needs an adjective to describe the noun *concern*. The question talks about the impact of increasing bee colony collapses. Since we are dependent on bee-pollinated agriculture, the concern must be serious. Of the answer choices only *grave* gives the meaning *serious*. (C) is the correct answer.

2. (C) The sentence contrasts the way Memorial Day Parade is being conducted this year with the way it was conducted in the previous years. The word *usually* indicates that this year there is a change. The blank must have an adjective that describes *affair* and provides an opposite meaning to *vulgar spectacle*. Of all the answer choices *solemn* fits the context. Thus (C) is the correct answer.

3. (C) This is a simple sentence. Focus on the second part of the sentence where the blank is. The blank needs a verb that describes an action done to *trouble* which cannot be *collaborated* or *designed* or *conducted*. It can only be *fomented*. Thus (C) is the correct answer.

4. (D) The policeman is describing an unknown man as someone who can beat a lie-detector. That means, the man has great skill in lying. Thus the blank must have a verb that means *to lie*. *Dissemble* is the synonym for *to lie* and thus (D) is the correct answer.

5. (A) The sentence describes Grant as a *man of few words*. He was a successful presidential candidate, so the blank must contain a synonym for a *man of few words*. *gregarious*, *loquacious* and *convivial* describe talkative people and the opposite of *a man of few words*. So (B), (C), (D) can be eliminated. *inarticulate* means the same as *a man of few words* and thus (A) is the correct answer.

6. (B) Any legislation passed by the labor movement is naturally expected to be for the benefit of the working class. So the blank needs a verb that means *to improve* the condition of the working class. Of the answer choices only *ameliorate* matches this meaning. Thus (B) is the correct answer.

7. (B) The blank needs a verb to describe an action police would do to robbers after a standoff of 36 hours. Since the police cannot *comprehend*, *dedicate* or *cadge* (*beg*) the robbers, they can only *apprehend* (*arrest*) them. Thus (B) is the correct answer.

8. (C) The central banks want to replace gold. Naturally they would want the replacement to have all the advantages of it (gold = yellow metal). Since there is a lack of such an alternate asset class, their attempt at replacement must not be a success. The blank needs a verb that means *failed* or *stopped*, *hindered* is the only answer choice that comes close to the meaning and fits the context. Thus (C) is the correct answer.

9. (D) All the answer choices are groups of people. The sentence describes a riot and the blank must be filled with a noun that describes people involved in the rioting. The sentence also says they are criminal elements. Of the four answer choices only *instigators* could mean people who are criminals and who would be involved in a riot. Thus (D) is the correct answer.

10. (A) The blank describes an action or attitude of Mark (something he is not hiding anymore). Since he is also planning not to work anymore (in the workplace) the attitude he is openly displaying must be negative toward the new management. (B), (C), and (D) describe positive attitudes toward the new management. Someone displaying those wouldn't have any fear and wouldn't be planning to quit. Someone who doesn't hide his *disdain* (a negative attitude) has no fear of retribution if he is already planning to quit. Thus (A) is the correct answer.

Sentence Completion (2 Blanks) Answers

SET 1		SET 2		SET 3		SET 4		SET 5	
Q No.	Answer	Q No.	Answer	Q No.	Answer	Q No.	Answer	Q No.	Answer
1	B	1	D	1	D	1	A	1	B
2	B	2	B	2	A	2	A	2	D
3	D	3	C	3	D	3	A	3	B
4	C	4	D	4	D	4	D	4	C
5	A	5	B	5	D	5	D	5	C
6	A	6	A	6	D	6	A	6	C
7	C	7	C	7	A	7	B	7	B
8	D	8	A	8	C	8	D	8	D
9	A	9	B	9	C	9	C	9	B
10	C	10	D	10	C	10	D	10	A

SET 6		SET 7		SET 8		SET 9		SET 10	
Q No.	Answer	Q No.	Answer	Q No.	Answer	Q No.	Answer	Q No.	Answer
1	B	1	B	1	A	1	B	1	C
2	B	2	A	2	A	2	B	2	B
3	C	3	A	3	D	3	D	3	A
4	B	4	D	4	D	4	A	4	D
5	C	5	C	5	B	5	C	5	B
6	D	6	C	6	B	6	B	6	C
7	A	7	B	7	C	7	B	7	B
8	A	8	B	8	C	8	A	8	C
9	D	9	D	9	A	9	D	9	A
10	C	10	A	10	B	10	B	10	A

SET 11		SET 12	
Q No.	Answer	Q No.	Answer
1	A	1	B
2	D	2	A
3	C	3	A
4	C	4	C
5	B	5	D
6	D	6	C
7	B	7	A
8	A	8	B
9	A	9	A
10	A	10	B

Detailed Explanations (2 Blanks) Set 1-5

EXPLANATIONS SET 1 (2 BLANKS)

1. (B) In this sentence, the second missing word is easier to spot than the first. The phrase 'rather than *oppose'*, coming immediately after the second missing word, implies that the second missing word must be an *antonym* of *oppose*. The only word among the choices for the second word which is an antonym of *oppose* is *complement* (meaning *be harmonious with)*. Its pair word *contrary* completes a logical sentence. So (B) is the answer.

2. (B) The expression "Even those who - must now -" indicates that the two missing words must have *opposite* meanings. Among the choices, the only pair of words which have opposite meanings are *"deny .... acknowledge"*. When inserted in the blanks in the sentence, these words lend a logical and cogent meaning to it. So, (B) is the answer.

3. (D) Here again, the second missing word is easier to spot. 'Looking for *connections* among *apparently* - data' indicates that the author is implying that the data, on first look, *do not appear to have any connections.* The missing word must therefore mean *disconnected.* Among the choices for the second missing word, it is *disparate* that has this meaning. *Paranoid* means a mental state in which one has a fixation that *there is conspiracy against him* all around. This word logically completes this ironic sentence, in which the author means that 'scientists think that nature is indulging in conspiracies against them, *hiding* the connections that they are looking for *in apparently disconnected data* '. So, (D) is the answer.

4. (C) The use of the phrase *'now, however'* immediately following the semi-colon means that the preceding missing word must mean the *opposite* of *'now'*. Among the choices for the first missing word, it is only the word 'initially' that can fit in here. "I support whatever actions my police chief takes" is in the nature of an *endorsement* of his actions. Thus, the pair of words in (C) completes a meaningful sentence.

5. (A) *'Escapist'* movies are those which have *no social message,* but are produced *purely for entertainment.* The phrase 'hence, most reviewers accepted escapist movies' shows that the reviewers appreciated the fact that the frightening nature of life during the depression left no option to the producers but to make escapist movies. The reviewers' acceptance of the escapist movies must therefore have been *without criticism.* Its pair 'realistically' is an appropriate choice for the first missing word, resulting in a meaningful sentence. So, (A) is the answer.

6. (A) Obviously, storms that cause floods and erosion cannot be described as *harmless* or *essential.* So, (C) can be easily eliminated on the basis of its suitability as the second

missing word. Since showers do not enable crops to *wither* or *parch,* (B) and (D) can be eliminated on the basis of their appropriateness for the first missing word. It is the pair of words *'flourish .... violent'* that gives a cogent meaning to the sentence. So, (A) is the answer.

7. (C) The importance of social and environmental costs in economic planning has been realized only recently. Therefore *conventional* (meaning *traditional; old-time*) measurements of an economy's performance are likely to have treated them as *unimportant,* or *ignored* them. Thus 'ignore' is the appropriate choice for the second missing word. Having ignored these *important* costs, the conventional measures are likely to give wrong or *misleading* results. Thus, the pair *'misleading .... ignore'* fits very well in the sentence, giving (C) as the answer.

8. (D) The appreciative word *distinguished* (to describe the person involved) implies that the movements that he refuses to ally with are *undesirable* ones. Among the choices for the second missing word, *sectarian* (meaning *serving the narrow interest of a small group*) is the only adjective describing an *undesirable* movement. Its pair word *independence* is one which justifies the *distinction* attributed to the person. So, (D) is the answer.

9. (A) The use of the conjunction *whereas* points to an inherent *contradiction* within the sentence. The sentence compares *popular* music with *classical* music. The phrase 'the *problem* with classical music' shows that the author has something *uncomplimentary* to say about classical music. Therefore, by contrast, what he says about popular music must be *complimentary* to it. The choice for the first missing word must therefore be restricted to *demonstrated* and *embellished.* The second missing word, in order to bring out the *contrast* in the sentence, must mean the exact *opposite* of *creativity* and *originality.* Among the choices, it is *'lack of innovation'* that means this. So, it is the pair *'demonstrated .... innovation'* that fits in well in the sentence and gives it a coherent meaning. So, (A) is the answer.

10. (C) *The word 'interstellar' means 'between stars'.* The sentence speaks of 'the scientific hypothesis that the expanses between the stars are devoid of matter'. A *discovery* can either *confirm* or *disprove* a hypothesis. Among the choices for the second missing word, *demolished* is the only word which has *one* of these meanings. The theory that the expanses between the stars are *devoid of* matter would certainly have been *demolished,* if it had been discovered that there are *molecules* in interstellar space. Thus *molecules,* the pair word of *demolished* fits in well to give a cogent meaning to the sentence. So, (C) is the answer.

EXPLANATIONS SET 2 (2 BLANKS)

1. (D) The use of the conjunction *though* indicates a *contradiction* within the sentence. The second missing word must therefore have a meaning which is the opposite of *a rival*. Among the choices, *friendly* is the most appropriate choice. Its pair word *analysis* completes a meaningful sentence "This subtle analysis of the senator's character, though crafted by a *friendly* hand, is as damaging as anything that a rival would have written". So, (D) is the answer.

2. (B) The use of the word *although* indicates an inherent contradiction in the sentence. The phrase 'the few works she did produce 'is a pointer that the first part must mean that she was not a very productive writer over. Among the choices for the first missing word, it is prolific that has this meaning. Its pair word mainstream (meaning common) is well-contrasted with avant-garde (meaning modern) poets, and fits in well in the second blank. So (B) is the answer.

3. (C) It is the word *curious* from which we should get the clue to the correct choice for the second missing word. The sentence means that most people are *shamelessly curious* about how the rich get their money and how they spend it. What will the *shamelessly curious* people do? They will try their best to *interlope,* either by *eavesdropping,* or *peeping through the hole,* or *reading others' letters* clandestinely. The only one among the choices for the first word which describes such a quality is *voyeurs* meaning 'peeping Toms'. Its pair word *insatiably* means *greedily,* and completes a meaningful sentence. So, (C) is the answer.

4. (D) The clue to the answer is in the conjunction *and so.* Therefore, the second part of the sentence must be a *logical consequence* of what is stated in the first part. The fact that rising state centralization is *detestable* cannot justify Luard's setting out a strategy for *modifying* it, *evaluating* it, *opposing* it, or *resisting* it. Therefore it is the first missing word that should logically explain why Luard is *not* setting out a strategy for taking *any of these actions.* Among the choices, it is the *inevitability* of rising state centralization which would make any of these actions *fruitless,* thereby explaining why Luard does not set out a strategy for any of those actions, especially *resisting* it, which is the pair word of *inevitable.* So, (D) is the answer.

5. (B) The use of the conjunction *despite* means that there is *an implied contrast* within the sentence. So, the pair of missing words must be *antonyms* of each other. Among the given choices, it is only the pair *expedient* (meaning *temporarily favorable)* and *liability* that are antonyms, whereas all the other pairs are *synonyms* of each other. So, (B) is the answer.

6. (A) A *conservative* designer would *conform to tradition* and will neither *flout* nor *ignore* it. So, (A) and (B) are the only possible choices for the second missing word.

Since no designer of an automobile will finalize a design which is *impractical,* (B) can be ruled out. *Striking,* meaning *totally different,* is the appropriate word for the first blank and it makes a cogent sentence along with *flout.* So, (A) is the answer.

7. (C) Puritans were highly religious Christians. So when they considered something as having been imposed by God's will, they would naturally try to do it *with devotion* and *to the best of their ability.* Among the given choices for the second missing word, 'conscientious *discharge* of the duties' brings out this meaning clearly. Its pair word *secular* (meaning *worldly),* fits in neatly in the sentence. So, (C) is the answer.

8. (A) China's is an ancient civilization, and so the country could not have had *bewilderment* or *ignorance* of medicinal plants for over 2000 years. The statement that the country had *affection* for medicinal plants is also quite absurd. So, even on consideration of the choices for the first missing word , *expertise in* is the only appropriate one. With its pair word lost, the sentence gets the cogent meaning though China has had expertise in medicinal plants for 2000 years, there was a period in its history when the art of herbal medicine had been almost lost. So, (A) is the answer.

9. (B) The single forceful word which represents the precaution of saving something *now* for meeting our requirement when it is *scarce* in the future, is *insurance.* This word is available in choice (B). Its pair word *hoard* which means *a saving for use in the future* also fits in very well in the sentence to give a cogent meaning to it. So, (B) is the answer.

10. (D) The information that the second part of the sentence imparts is that there exists a natural human desire to celebrate and decorate, and to take delight in ornament. If modern architecture is 'elaborate', it would be *fulfilling,* and not *neglecting,* this desire. So, (A) is wrong. If modern architecture is 'austere', it would be *neglecting* this natural desire, and not *recognizing* it. So, (B) is wrong. If modern architecture 'embellishes', it would again be *fulfilling* this natural desire, and not be *undermining* it. So, (C) is also wrong. If modern architecture is 'severe' *(meaning* 'austere'), it would be *opposing* this natural desire. So, (D) leads to a logical sentence, and is the answer.

EXPLANATIONS SET 3 (2 BLANKS)

1. (D) The phrase "inviting a *chuckle,* perhaps, but certainly not a ..... " implies that the second missing word is a *stronger reaction* than *a chuckle* (meaning a *giggle; a smile)*. Among the choices *guffaw* (meaning *loud laughter)* is the only word having this meaning. Its pair word *humorous* completes a meaningful sentence. So. (D) is the answer.

2. (A) The use of the semi-colon to divide the two parts of the sentence implies that the second part is *a logical continuation* of what is stated in the first part. The first part says that human beings are *much less creatures of instinct* than other animals are. So, our behavior patterns must have *less to do with instinct* than the animals', and must be based on *reason* or *training.* Among the choices for the first missing word, *learned* is the only word which has this meaning. Its pair word *inherited* fits in well in the phrase *'learned* rather than *inherited'* to give a cogent meaning to the sentence. So, (A) is the answer.

3. (D) The use of the word *although* shows that there is a *contradiction* of sense within the sentence. If the troops had fought bravely, a General would normally *press forward,* and enforce a defeat on the enemy. The use of the conjunction *although* must imply the *exact opposite,* namely, that the General himself faced defeat. Among the choices for the first missing word, *acknowledge* is the only word that suits the sentence. If he apprehended *defeat,* he would naturally *order* his troops to retreat so that they could regroup later. So, the pair of words in (D) completes a meaningful sentence, and is the answer.

4 (D) The sentence describes the imagination of the writer as a torrent (meaning an uncontrolled flood). By not publishing his writings hastily the author must have allowed it either to abate or subside (both meaning to become less strong). Both these words are suitable to fill the first blank. Of the two choices for the second missing word, it is only the phrase 'novelties of this creation' that make sense in the sentence. So, (D) is the answer.

5. (D) The phrase '- or childish' implies that the missing word must be a *synonym* of *childish.* Among the given choices, *trivial* is nearest in meaning to *childish.* From the phrases 'aggression *of* profanity' and 'assault *on* -', we can infer that the missing word here must be *an antonym* of *profanity* (meaning *obscenity; vulgarism). Decorum,* the pair word of *childish* has this meaning, and fits in well in the sentence. So, (D) is the answer.

6. (D) When a person suddenly loses consciousness, a *bystander* (who may not be a doctor) should be expected to administer him *first aid* till medical attention is made available to the patient. The bystander cannot be expected to precipitate or *predict* or *detect* the effects of the problem, but *to take action to nullify* the effects of the problem. The word *counter* means the same as *to attempt to nullify,* and is the only one among the

choices for the second missing word which has this meaning. Its pair word *diagnose* completes a meaningful sentence, because a mere *bystander* cannot be expected to be able to *diagnose* a medical problem. So, (D) is the answer.

7. (A) The statement that the stories of the marvels were *ultimately based on historical fact* means that they were not purely imaginary, implying that they were partly fictitious and partly factual. It is the phrase *partly factual* which has been expressed negatively in the second part of the sentence as *'they did not actually -'*. Among the choices for the second missing word, it is only *invent* which is appropriate for this blank. Its pair word *embroidered* (meaning *embellished*) completes a logical sentence. So, (A) is the answer.

8. (C) The phrase *'subtly* persuasive arguments' implies that the arguments of Fuentes were quite logical, but were *in low key*. So, they cannot be said to *implore'* (meaning *'to beg earnestly')*, or *to command*, readers to do something. So, (A) and (D) can be ruled out on a consideration of the choices for the first missing word. So, the only possible choices for the first missing word are *condition* and *invite*. The arguments for the *continuity* of a people's culture must mean that their future cannot be *separated from* their past. Among the remaining choices *inferred* and *divorced* for the second missing word, it is the latter that means this, and is the answer. The pair of words in (C) *'invite .... divorced'* lends a logical meaning to the given sentence, and is the answer.

9. (C) The author asserts that the principle of equality should not imply a *leveling down*, meaning that some differences are *inevitable* and must be *allowed to continue*. Human needs cannot be said to be *universal*, since what, a *child* requires is different from what an *adult* requires, and what an *Eskimo* requires is different what *a man in the tropics* requires. So, (A) is incorrect. Similarly *impudence* (meaning *rashness)*, and *inequity* (meaning *injustice)* are not appropriate words to describe the human needs . Since human needs are many and different, it is plurality which is the most appropriate choice for the first missing word. Its pair word diverse (meaning many; different) completes a meaningful sentence. So, (C) is the answer.

10. (C) If quantitative laws turn out to be the *same* for *similar* phenomena, there would be nothing *unsuspected* about such results. So, the second missing word must mean the opposite of *similar*. Among the choices for the second missing word, *dissimilar* is the only choice with this meaning. Its pair word *relationships* completes a logical sentence. So, (C) is the answer.

EXPLANATIONS SET 4 (2 BLANKS)

1. (A) The clue to the answer to this question lies in the very first part of the sentence, namely, 'All he ever wanted was *his own way'*. This means that the person described was always particular *in achieving whatever he wanted* or in *achieving his aim or goal.* So, (A) is the answer. Even otherwise, is not the very definition of victory 'the *achievement* of the *goal'*?

2. (A) Microbiologists are scientists who study microorganisms such as bacteria, viruses and germs. Obviously, these organisms, in their appearance, are not *homogeneous* (meaning *uniform*), or *erratic* (meaning *irregular*), or *conspicuous* (meaning *readily noticeable*). So, among the choices for the first missing word, *diverse* (meaning *dissimilar*) is the only appropriate expression. Its pair word fits in well in the phrase 'so *diverse* in appearance and habits as to *belie* the common bond presumed to ally them'. So, (A) is the answer.

3. (A) The clue to the correct answer lies in the last line 'earthworks and roads *buried beneath the fields'.* Now, which is the science (among the four given choices for the first missing word) which deals with things *buried underground? Archaeology,* of course! The pair of words in (A), when fitted into the sentence, give it a cogent meaning. So, (A) is the answer.

4. (D) The phrase *in addition to* in the beginning of the sentence shows that there is *no contradiction* within the sentence, and the second half of the sentence *corroborates* the first half. The attitude of the governor towards the legislature should therefore have been based on his *natural predilection for* (meaning *inclination towards*) compromise. Among the choices for the first blank, the only phrase which indicates a *compromising* attitude is *conciliatory toward.* Its pair word *isolation* suits the second blank quite well to give us a sentence with a cogent meaning. So, (D) is the answer.

5. (D) *(Schizophrenia* is the scientific term for *split personality traits)*. Systematic studies cannot *challenge* or *enhance* answers, but can only *clarify* or *yield* answers. So, (B) and (C) are ruled out on a consideration of the suitability of the choices for the first missing word itself. The *not only but also* conjunction in the sentence implies 'differentiated' and 'limited' lend a logical meaning to the consonance of ideas in the sentence. If the question had given the sentence '*been completely formulated,*' it is not likely that systematic studies would have failed to clarify the answers. So the pair word of clarify does not result in a logical sentence. But, if the question itself had been *incorrectly* formulated it is logical that the systematic studies would have failed to *yield* the answers. Thus the pair of words in (D) completes a logical and meaningful sentence, and is the answer.

6. (A) Normally, in a coin-flipping experiment, coins are expected to fall either *heads up* or *tails up*. What can one do when, in an extraordinary case, the flipped coin *stands on its edge,* making it an *ambiguous* case? One logical step is *to ignore* this case. Its pair word 'classification' (In this case, the classification was that only two categories - heads up or tails up - were considered possible.) completes a meaningful sentence. So, (A) is the answer.

7. (B) The first missing word has been elaborated in the second part of the sentence as 'permitting us to do *by degrees'.* Among the choices *anger, gradualism, apathy,* and *fanaticism* for this word, it is only *gradualism* which has a nexus to doing something *by degrees.* So, even from the point of view of the first missing word, we can choose (B) as the only possible answer. Its pair phrase *shrink from* (meaning *avoid completely*) completes a meaningful sentence, confirming the correctness of this choice.

8. (D) The last phrase ' between *professed and genuine* beliefs' indicates that the missing word here must be the one which means that the *professed* (meaning *openly declared*) and the *genuine* (meaning *real*) beliefs are *not the same,* but are *different.* Among the choices for the second missing word, only *discrepancy* and *dissonance* have this meaning. So, we can restrict our further examination to (C) and (D). If there is a *discrepancy* or *dissonance* between the *professed* and the *actual* beliefs of people, our *initial* comprehension of the assumptions by which people act cannot be *confirmed* by such a *discrepancy* or *dissonance,* but can only be *modified* by it. So, from the point of view of the second missing word, it is only (D) which is suitable, and is the answer.

9. (C) *Predators* (meaning *hunting animals*) will not be *lured* or *encouraged* by traps, poison and shotguns. So, (A) and (D) are ruled out even on the basis of their suitability for the first missing word. If predators are *destroyed* by traps, poison and shotguns, and therefore *cease to feast* on flocks of sheep, there is no need for the use of the conjunction *although* in the sentence. So, (B) is wrong. So it is the pair of words *'impeded. continue'* which give a cogent meaning to the given sentence. So, (C) is the answer.

10. (D) The use of the verb *contrasts* implies that the two missing adjectives of the same word *vocabulary* must be *antonyms* of each other. Of the choices, *nuanced* and *subtle* are synonyms; *uninformative* and *misleading* are synonyms; *euphemistic* and *abstract,* though not *synonyms,* have *similar connotations;* and *technical* and *jargon-laden* are also synonyms. It is the phrases *highly differentiated vocabulary* and *limited vocabulary* which form antonyms of each other. So (D) is the only possible answer.

EXPLANATIONS SET 5 (2 BLANKS)

1. (B) The first missing word must have the same relationship to athletic events as *museum goers* have to *paintings*. Why do people go to the museum? To *see* paintings, obviously. Among the choices, *stadiums* is the only place. So, even from the point of view of the first missing word, we can choose (B) as the only possible answer.

2. (D) All the four choices for the first missing word can meaningfully fill the blank in the phrase 'It is ..... to maintain'. So, we should look for a clue to the correct answer in the last part of the sentence. The phrase 'every *departure* from that order constitutes a .... of a natural law' implies that the missing word here must be a synonym of *departure*. Among the given choices, it is only *transgression* and *violation* which have this meaning. Since there is no natural law for governing sentence order, a departure from the norm is normal and cannot be a violation . So, (B) is not the answer. It would certainly be *unjustifiable* to maintain that every departure from that order constitutes a *violation* of a natural law.

3. (B) The first part of the sentence implies that the book's *credibility* (meaning *believability; trustworthiness*) is being stretched beyond limit, "with a *slender* web of evidence on one salient point having to support .... of implications". Among the choices for the second missing word, *'a vast superstructure* of implications', *'a vast array* of implications' and *'a vast network* of implications' all make sense in this context. So, (B), (C) and (D) are all possible answers *from the point of view of the second missing word.* Among the corresponding phrases that result from the choice of their pair words for the first missing word . 'the slender, *though far from nonexistent,* web of evidence', makes the most logical sense and so, (B) is the answer.

4. (C) The use of the phrase 'and so' as the conjunction means that the second part of the sentence must *corroborate* the first. The first part of the sentence says that important stages of evolution occurred in tropical countries *where it is difficult to explore for fossils*. Therefore the discovery of fossils *pertinent to evolution* must be *rare*. Among the choices, only *unique* and *uncommon* are the suitable words for the first missing word. The pair word of *unique* is *resulted,* but the phrase 'and so their discovery *has resulted'* does not make sense in the sentence. On the contrary, the phrase 'and so their discovery *has lagged* (meaning *has slowed down)'* makes eminent sense in the context. So, (C) is the answer.

5. (C) The second part of the sentence means that imagination not only *destroys and alters,* but also '- *isolated* beliefs, insights and mental habits *into strongly unified systems'*. Among the choices for the second missing word, those that mean the conversion of *isolated* beliefs into *strongly unified* systems is only *fuses*. So, our search for the answer gets limited to (C). If imagination *fuses* isolated beliefs into strongly unified systems, it will be an error to regard it as a mainly *revolutionary* force. So, the pair of words in (C) completes a meaningful sentence, and is the answer.

6. (C) What the sentence apparently implies is that our gradual introduction to the world of a novel (which is initially *strange* to us) is similar to the gradual *orientation* (meaning *adjustment*) of an infant to the physical world. So, *introduction* and *adjustment* are the only possible choices for the second missing word, limiting our further examination to (B) or (C). The phrase "our gradual and selective orientation to its manners *completes* infants' introduction to their environment" does not make any sense. So, (B) can be discarded. With the pair of words in (C), we get the sentence, "our gradual and selective orientation to its manners *resembles* infants' introduction to their environment" which makes eminent sense. So, (C) is the answer.

7. (B) The second missing word in the phrase 'has become less ……..' should substantiate the phrase that follows it: 'taking the form of *inertia* rather than *direct attack*'. *Aggressive* is the only word among the choices for the second word that fits in here. Its pair word, *institutionalized,* which means *formally established* completes a meaningful sentence. So, (B) is the answer.

8. (D) The second part of the sentence means that the style adopted by Rousseau in his discussion of the physical sciences *deviated* from the *cautious* and *unadorned prose* of the day. So, the second missing word must mean the *opposite* of *cautious and unadorned.* Among the choices, it is only *unrestrained* that has this meaning when we re-read the sentence along with its pair phrase …..*unrestrained* discussion of the physical sciences', which is an eminently logical sentence. So (D) is the answer.

9. (B) The use of the phrase *neither - nor* implies that the first missing word must imply the *opposite* of the phrase *condescends to them* (meaning *patronizes them from a superior position).* Among the given choices for the second missing word, *inflates* and *admires* are the only two which are the opposites of *condescends*. Choosing (D) first, we get the sentence as, "A truly *reverent* historian of science, Meyer neither *admires* the abilities of the scientists she presents …. ", which is *self-contradictory*. The pair of words in (B) give the sentence, "A truly *objective* (meaning *dispassionate*) historian of science, Meyer neither *inflates* the abilities of the scientists she presents nor *condescends to* them", which forms a logical statement. So, (B) is the answer.

10. (A) An animal which is *losing* in a struggle cannot save itself from destruction by an act of *hostility* (because the struggle implies that there is already hostility and it is losing in it), or by an act of *bluffing,* or by an act of *anger,* or by an act of *hatred.* It can sometimes save itself by an act of *submission,* especially when such submission is recognized and *accepted* by the winner. Thus, the pair of words in (A) completes a meaningful sentence, and is the answer.

SYNONYMS

Synonym Strategies

All synonym questions have a stem word, followed by 4 answer choices. Your task is to select the answer choice which is closest in meaning to the stem word.

There are some simple strategies you can follow:

Strategy 1 – When you know the stem word

When you know the stem word, cover the answer choices and then think of a word, phrase or definition closest in meaning to the stem word. Then, look for that word or a similar word, among the answer choices.

Let us look at the following example:

PATRONIZE (stem word)

(A) beautify

(B) army

(C) fight

(D) condescend

You may have heard this word used in the context of "I don't need your criticism. Don't **patronize** me." So, you may understand that it has a negative connotation. You may, through context, understand the definition of "PATRONIZE" as being *looking down on* someone. Look for the word that is closest in meaning to the expression *to look down on*.

The word that is closest in meaning to this phrase is (D) condescend, which is the correct answer.

Another example:

VULNERABLE (stem word)

(A) tired

(B) strong

(C) capable

(D) fragile

Of course, it is highly likely that you know the word "VULNERABLE". So, try to think of a word or phrase that may be closest in meaning to the word "VULNERABLE". You may come up with *easily hurt*, and so while examining the answer choices, you can discern that answer choice (D) fragile is closest in meaning. Therefore, the correct answer choice is (D) fragile.

Strategy 2 – When you do not know the stem word

When you do not know the stem word, try to think of the context in which the stem word is used. Maybe you have heard or read the word before.

Let us look at the following example:

AUDACITY (stem word)

(A) disappointment

(B) noise

(C) perfect

(D) aggression

If you come across a word that you do not know, in this case, "AUDACITY", then it is very important to think of the *context* in which it is used.

You may have heard or read the expression, "Oh! The audacity of that child!" expressing criticism towards the behavior of that child. So, we understand that the stem word is related to behavior. Therefore, we can rule out answer choice (A) disappointment and answer choice (B) noise as these two words are not close in meaning to the stem word.

Answer choice (C) perfect has a positive connotation and we know that "AUDACITY" has a negative connotation, in other words, it means something negative, so we can also rule out answer choice (C).

Therefore, the correct answer is (D) aggression.

Another example:

ALLEVIATE (stem word)

(A) simplify

(B) harden

(C) change

(D) ease

You may not know the meaning of the word "ALLEVIATE", but you may have heard or seen it used in a sentence.

For example, "The doctor tried to **alleviate** the patient's pain".

As you can logically deduce, the doctor is trying to make the patient's pain go away.

So, upon examining the answer options, you would immediately eliminate choice (B), because it does not make sense in this context.

Also answer choices (A) simplify and (C) change are not close in meaning to this particular word or context. Hence, the correct answer, we can conclude, is (D) ease.

If you are unsure of the correct meaning of a word, try to remember where you may have heard or seen that word before, i.e. in which context. So, let us look at another example:

FIGURATIVE (stem word)

(A) serious

(B) fantastic

(C) metaphoric

(D) literal

Looking at the word "FIGURATIVE", you should try to recall where you have heard or seen this word before.

Perhaps, in your English class, your teacher used "figurative language" to describe certain literary devices, such as symbols or metaphors.

Thus, recalling this context helps a lot as you may understand that answer (C) metaphoric is closest in meaning to "FIGURATIVE".

Strategy 3 – Positive, Negative or Neutral

If a stem word is positive, then the answer choice must be positive. If a stem word is negative, then the answer choice must be negative as well. If the word is neutral, then the answer choice must be neutral. Let us look at this example:

CORRUPT (stem word)

(A) dishonest   -

(B) belittle   -

(C) remove   N

(D) portray   N

You should try to understand whether "CORRUPT" is a positive, negative or neutral word.

If we look at the stem word and try to figure out in which context it is used, whether we have seen or heard it before, we may remember that it has to do with something immoral.

For example: "The referee was corrupt as he broke the rules of the tennis tournament."

So, now that you know that the stem word has negative connotations, Choices (C) remove and (D) portray are both neutral words so this means that they can be eliminated.

We are left with two choices, (A) and (B) which have negative connotations.

Based on the contextual sentence (*corrupt referee….*), you can eliminate answer choices (B), arriving at the conclusion that (A) dishonest is the correct answer choice.

Let us look at another example:

ENHANCE (stem word)

(A) broaden N

(B) worsen -

(C) arrange N

(D) improve +

We can start by determining whether "ENHANCE" has a positive, negative or neutral connotation. You may have heard or seen the word before in context, for example, "You can enhance the taste of the sauce by using fresh ingredients".

So, you may understand that it is related *to making something taste better*, or *to better*. So, "ENHANCE" is a word with a POSITIVE connotation.

Since the stem word is positive, the correct answer choice will also be positive. We can put a + sign next to the words we deem positive, a – sign next to the words we deem negative and an N next to the neutral ones.

The only positive answer choice is (D) improve and is the correct answer.

Strategy 4 – Word Parts

Word parts can give you powerful clues to figure out the meaning of words. Prefixes come at the beginning of the word, suffixes come at the end of a word and the root can be in any part of the word. Let us look at the following example:

CHARISMATIC (stem word)

(A) troublesome

(B) peculiar

(C) charming

(D) skill

Let us look at the stem word "CHARISMATIC". You may have heard this word before as in "A charismatic leader", for example. You can see that "charismatic" is actually an adjective as it describes the noun "leader". So, the correct answer choice will also be an adjective.

It also has a positive connotation, so you would be looking for an answer choice with a positive connotation. Upon examining the answer choices, therefore, you can eliminate (D) skill as it is a noun. You can also eliminate (A) troublesome and (B) peculiar as these words have a negative connotation. Therefore, the correct answer choice is (C) charming.

Another example:

TRIATHLON (stem word)

(A) dancer

(B) brawl

(C) sport

(D) party

When looking at the word "TRIATHLON", you may notice the prefix "TRI" which means *three*. You may also notice that the second syllable "ATHLON" is similar to *athlete*. The triathlon is actually a sport event that consists of three sports trials. So, the word closest in meaning to "TRIATHLON" would be (C) sport.

VERB, NOUN, ADJECTIVE OR ADVERB

The elimination process can be pushed forward by actually determining whether the stem word is a verb, noun, adjective or adverb. If the stem word is a verb, then the correct answer choice will also be a verb, for example.

Thus, the part of speech of the stem word corresponds to the part of speech of the answer choice.

Let us look at the example below:

BENEFICIAL (stem word)

(A) bad luck   -

(B) helpful   +

(C) blessing   +

(D) sorrow   -

You may associate the word "BENEFICIAL" with *benefit*, meaning something positive. After having indicated whether each answer choice has a positive or a negative connotation, we are left with two choices that are positive.

Choice (C) blessing is ruled out because "blessing" is a noun, whereas "BENEFICIAL" is an adjective.

So, by elimination, we have the correct answer, which is (B) helpful.

Of course, "helpful" is an adjective, as is "BENEFICIAL".

Strategy 5 – Beware of Attractors

Attractors are words designed to distract you from the correct answer choice so that you may choose a 'correct sounding/looking' answer, but which would actually be the wrong choice.

The first thing to do is to try to ANTICIPATE the answer, if you know the stem word. If the stem word is familiar to you, try to come up with a simple definition of your own before looking at the answer choices.

Let us look at the following example:

EVACUATE (stem word)

(A) institute

(B) fill

(C) maintenance

(D) empty

It may be that students confuse the stem word "EVACUATE" with answer choice (A) institute because you may have heard the phrase "The institute was evacuated."

However, this answer choice is an attractor, listed to distract your attention, and is not the correct answer.

"EVACUATE" is a verb, hence the correct answer choice must also be a verb. Answer choices (A) institute and (C) maintenance are thus eliminated as they are both nouns.

Another important point is the root of the word which, you may understand is "vacant", therefore, answer choices (B) fill can also be eliminated as it is not close in meaning to the root. Therefore, the correct answer is (D) empty.

Here is one more example:

AMIABLE (stem word)

(A) talkative

(B) friendly

(C) aggressive

(D) amnesty

You may also notice answer choice (D) "amnesty" is an attractor as it begins with the same two letters "am". But, "amnesty" is a noun, whereas "AMIABLE" is an adjective.

Hence, answer (D) is incorrect.

Try not to jump to conclusions and think that you already know the answer because you will likely make a mistake.

Before being drawn to an attractor, think of the context of the word. You may have heard or read the stem word before. For example, "The student was quite amiable and easy to get along with."

This may lead you to think that "AMIABLE" is similar to choice (A) "talkative" (which, is another attractor), but you would be wrong!

The correct answer choice is in fact (B) friendly.

Strategy 6 – Strategy Combination

Use all of the strategies to help you eliminate. Let us look at the following example:

EXCAVATE (stem word)

(A) infect   -

(B) display   N

(C) pardon   +

(D) uncover N

The prefix "EX" means *exit* and the root word "CAV" means *hole*, using Strategy 4 – Word Parts. Also, using Strategy 3 – Positive or Negative, you can also figure out whether "EXCAVATE" is a positive or negative word or whether it is neutral in meaning. "EXCAVATE" is a neutral word. So, the answer choice will be neutral.

We can eliminate answer choice (A) infect, which is a negative word. We can also eliminate choice (C) pardon which is a positive words. So, we are left with answer choice (B) display and answer choice (D) uncover and the choice closest in meaning to exit is uncover so the correct answer choice is **(D) uncover.**

You may notice how we used a combination of strategies to arrive at the correct answer.

Another example:

OMINOUS (stem word)

(A) dismal   -

(B) stunning +

(C) hurtful   -

(D) threatening -

Looking at the stem word, try to see if you can determine the root of the word. You may see that "OMINOUS" comes from "omen" which means a sign, and it has a negative connotation.

Therefore, you would need to determine which of the answer choices have a positive, negative or neutral connotation.

Upon examining the answer choices, choices (A) dismal, (C) hurtful and (D) threatening are negative, while choice (B) stunning is positive.

So, choice (B) can be eliminated.

Now, try not to be swayed or distracted by the attractors (A) dismal and (C) hurtful which may be associated with *omen* or *ominous*, but are provided to distract your attention and are not the correct choice, hence can be eliminated.

The correct answer choice is (D) threatening.

Now, try to answer the following review exercises on your own, taking into consideration the strategies and tips we have discussed so far:

Synonyms Practice Set 1 - 30

SYNONYMS SET 1

Select the word that is closest in meaning to the capitalized word.

1. DICHOTOMY
A) duality   B) denouncement   C) delivery   D) confusion

2. FIDUCIARY
A) announcer   B) trustee   C) competitor   D) conservative

3. DESSICATE
A) thirsty   B) vacuum   C) dry   D) burnt

4. DIAPHANOUS
A) opaque   B) colorful   C) fashionable   D) transparent

5. MORIBUND
A) immortal   B) potent   C) potential   D) stagnant

6. QUANDARY
A) hazard   B) closet   C) suspicion   D) predicament

7. DIURNAL
A) nocturnal   B) habitual   C) enduring   D) daily

8. GREGARIOUS
A) large   B) egregious   C) friendly   D) flagrant

9. EPHEMERAL
A) pristine   B) exquisite   C) flexible   D) transient

10. FACILE
A) impressive   B) versatile   C) decisive   D) superficial

11. FULSOME
A) abundant   B) incessant   C) obscene   D) handsome

12. LANGUISH
A) devastate   B) deteriorate   C) refuse   D) imprison

13. PALLOR
A) luster B) shape C) paleness D) sanguine

14. PERFIDY
A) loyalty B) faithful C) obedience D) treachery

15. EFFIGY
A) likeness B) smoke C) fire D) mural

16. GRATUITOUS
A) inexpensive B) reasonable C) uncalled for D) appreciative

17. DESULTORY
A) hot B) aimless C) uncontrolled D) principled

18. IMMUTABLE
A) loud B) imminent C) fixed D) premature

19. ANATHEMA
A) rare B) exclusive C) slanderous D) curse

20. OBDURATE
A) preventive B) clueless C) stubborn D) accessible

21. PROGENITOR
A) precursor B) witness C) guardian D) organizer

22. SUBTERFUGE
A) plan B) trickery C) treason D) excuse

23. INGRATIATE
A) explain B) join C) curry favor D) deliver

24. AKIN
A) painful B) parallel C) remote D) similar

25. CHRONIC
A) punctual B) persistent C) deplorable D) record

26. EPITHET
A) label B) defense C) addendum D) postscript

SYNONYMS SET 2

Select the word that is closest in meaning to the capitalized word.

1. SURFEIT
A) excess   B) lack   C) numerical   D) surrender

2. USURP
A) inherit   B) seize   C) allocate   D) remove

3. ABYSMAL
A) disturbing   B) uninspired   C) awful   D) plunging

4. PROSCRIBE
A) advocate   B) recommend   C) govern   D) ban

5. BASTION
A) stronghold   B) provision   C) patron   D) banner

6. INGENUOUS
A) clever   B) naive   C) inspired   D) authentic

7. VIVACIOUS
A) strange   B) lively   C) beautiful   D) relatable

8. ALTRUISM
A) greatness   B) selflessness   C) honesty   D) truthfulness

9. AUSTERE
A) wasteful   B) confusing   C) financial   D) simple

10. CHAGRIN
A) pleasure   B) expectation   C) surprise   D) disappointment

11. CORPULENT
A) obese   B) obscene   C) comfortable   D) dead

12. ELEGY
A) agreement   B) will   C) lament   D) document

13. EGRESS
A) elevate B) proceed C) continue D) exit

14. EPITOME
A) extract B) tiny C) example D) advance

15. FALLACY
A) delusion B) logic C) blasphemy D) prejudice

16. DOCTRINE
A) belief B) treatment C) speech D) partition

17. INANE
A) clever B) absurd C) stunted D) reasonable

18. INSIPID
A) rapid B) fearless C) dull D) neutral

19. MOROSE
A) combative B) childish C) normal D) sullen

20. OPULENT
A) fat B) prosperous C) timid D) liberal

21. DROSS
A) junk B) larder C) target D) piece

22. PARSIMONIOUS
A) herbal B) miserly C) prudent D) adept

23. RECALCITRANT
A) subordinate B) measurable C) rebellious D) unbound

24. PILFER
A) pawn B) steal C) admit D) absorb

25. RETICENT
A) pent up B) reserved C) vapid D) remorseful

26. VENERATION
A) applause B) worship C) entertainment D) removal

SYNONYMS SET 3

Select the word that is closest in meaning to the capitalized word.

1. NEBULOUS
A) spatial B) vague ✓ C) shiny D) complex

2. PROGNOSTICATE
A) delay ✓ B) predict C) explain D) discover

3. SKINFLINT
A) lanky B) stubborn C) cheap D) fitting

4. OSTENTATIOUS
A) murky B) proud C) greedy ✓ D) flashy

5. ADAGE
A) ancient B) stone C) book D) proverb

6. ADJUNCT
A) inbuilt B) assistant C) superior D) similar

7. ADVERSARY
A) ally B) opponent ✓ C) boast D) difficulty

8. AFFABLE
A) inexpensive B) genial C) comedic ✓ D) clingy

9. AFFECTATION
A) preference B) liking ✓ C) impact D) pretense

10. ALLEVIATE
A) fertile B) raise C) relieve ✓ D) increase

11. ALLURE
A) greed B) attraction ✓ C) gravity D) beauty

12. AMOROUS
A) powdery B) white C) romantic D) successful

13. AMORPHOUS
A) flirty	B) earthy	C) formless	D) porous

14. ANOINT
A) leverage	B) smear	C) dedicate	D) praise

15. ANIMOSITY
A) hatred	B) belief	C) connection	D) intensity

16. ANTIDOTE
A) remedy	B) dislike	C) care	D) venom

17. APERTURE
A) limb	B) hole	C) alignment	D) valley

18. AQUEOUS
A) acidic	B) solid	C) gaseous	D) watery

19. ARID
A) like	B) eliminate	C) vast	D) dry

20. ARTIFICE
A) produce	B) knowledge	C) plan	D) trick

21. BANAL
A) stale	B) hole	C) fruity	D) defective

22. BEGUILE
A) beauty	B) deceive	C) innocence	D) start

23. BELLIGERENCE
A) volume	B) arrogance	C) hostility	D) reluctance

24. BENEVOLENCE
A) attraction	B) advantage	C) greed	D) kindness

25. BOISTEROUS
A) manly	B) toxic	C) immobile	D) noisy

26. BRAVADO
A) bluster	B) sorrow	C) consideration	D) curse

SYNONYMS SET 4

Select the word that is closest in meaning to the capitalized word.

1. ECLECTIC
A) broad   B) loud   C) creaky   D) excited

2. CAPRICE
A) decision   B) whim   C) knot   D) problem

3. CASCADE
A) effect   B) aid   C) spurt   D) enforce

4. CATASTROPHE
A) feline   B) reward   C) disaster   D) sample

5. CELESTIAL
A) silent   B) divine   C) roomy   D) spatial

6. CHASM
A) happiness   B) gap   C) volley   D) width

7. CHOLERIC
A) diseased   B) irritable   C) weak   D) infectious

8. CIRCUMSCRIBE
A) revolve   B) rotate   C) restrict   D) etch

9. CONTENTIOUS
A) belonging   B) explainable   C) assertive   D) combative

10. COPIOUS
A) plenty   B) tasty   C) fluid   D) alike

11. COUNTENANCE
A) expression   B) finite   C) numeric   D) obscure

12. DAWDLE
A) scribble   B) linger   C) fish   D) walk

13. DEADLOCK
A) fatal   B) eliminate   C) stall   D) secure

14. DEARTH
A) kindness   B) abundance   C) sympathy   D) lack

15. DELUGE
A) desire   B) flood   C) rise   D) disaster

16. DESOLATION
A) gloom   B) removal   C) scarcity   D) hostility

17. DESTITUTE
A) implement   B) poor   C) replace   D) offer

18. DINGY
A) crooked   B) narrow   C) dark   D) smelly

19. DISCURSIVE
A) repeated   B) rambling   C) pathetic   D) linear

20. DOFF
A) scratch   B) wear   C) remove   D) replace

21. DOGMATIC
A) pleasing   B) canine   C) opinionated   D) relaxed

22. ECCENTRIC
A) circular   B) strange   C) flat   D) dashing

23. ECSTATIC
A) drugged   B) sluggish   C) elated   D) critical

24. EDDY
A) tense   B) nervous   C) content   D) vortex

25. ELUSIVE
A) bitter   B) lengthy   C) slippery   D) special

26. BREVITY
A) shortness   B) happiness   C) boast   D) mirth

SYNONYMS SET 5

Select the word that is closest in meaning to the capitalized word.

1. ERUDITE
A) learned   B) ancient   C) stubborn   D) weak

2. ETIQUETTE
A) commands   B) manners   C) instructions   D) decoration

3. EXOTIC
A) romantic   B) known   C) strange   D) closed

4. EXPUNGE
A) throw   B) frame   C) clear   D) erase

5. ENDEAVOR
A) remove   B) brag   C) try   D) add

6. FATIGUE
A) tiredness   B) destiny   C) death   D) flaw

7. FAUNA
A) plant   B) life   C) steam   D) animal

8. FELICITY
A) agony   B) swiftness   C) pleasure   D) luck

9. FERVENT
A) frequent   B) provocative   C) unsteady   D) passionate

10. FICKLE
A) steady   B) inconsistent   C) predictable   D) curved

11. FLAGRANT
A) blatant   B) aromatic   C) angular   D) routine

12. GARRULOUS
A) coarse   B) talkative   C) irritable   D) unsteady

13. GERMINATE
A) spread B) infect C) grow D) check

14. GLIB
A) edible B) full C) silent D) smooth

15. GROTESQUE
A) large B) ordinary C) detested D) ugly

16. HALLOWED
A) blessed B) shallow C) depressed D) empty

17. HARBINGER
A) unique B) harm C) death D) sign

18. HETEROGENEOUS
A) similar B) uniform C) different D) brilliant

19. HIBERNATE
A) retreat B) attack C) escape D) sleep

20. HOVEL
A) village B) hut C) spade D) hamlet

21. IMMACULATE
A) heavenly B) clean C) scholarly D) doubtless

22. IMMINENT
A) prominent B) close C) avoidable D) important

23. IMPASSE
A) elevation B) passion C) standstill D) junction

24. IMPERVIOUS
A) previous B) predictable C) flexible D) resistant

25. IMPIOUS
A) ungodly B) adorable C) obedient D) smelly

26. INADVERTENT
A) unintentional B) purposeful C) expected D) skillful

SYNONYMS SET 6

Select the word that is closest in meaning to the capitalized word.

1. IRATE
A) furious   B) rated   C) standardized   D) displeased

2. JEER
A) look   B) mock   C) shout   D) tremble

3. JUDICIOUS
A) punishable   B) rounded   C) reasonable   D) sharp

4. KINETIC
A) potential   B) immobile   C) limp   D) dynamic

5. LAGOON
A) weapon   B) wave   C) surface   D) pool

6. LIMBER
A) weak   B) flexible   C) sharp   D) young

7. MAGNANIMOUS
A) large   B) generous   C) victorious   D) invincible

8. MALFUNCTION
A) harm   B) rot   C) fault   D) evil

9. MALLEABLE
A) popular   B) attractive   C) shiny   D) flexible

10. MAR
A) clear   B) frame   C) ruin   D) signify

11. MELANCHOLY
A) confusion   B) elation   C) gloom   D) indecision

12. MINUSCULE
A) swift   B) tiny   C) null   D) close

13. MURKY
A) lucky   B) windy   C) confusing   D) stormy

14. GILDED
A) gifted   B) famous   C) cursed   D) wealthy

15. NIMBLE
A) biting   B) quick   C) young   D) lean

16. SEEP
A) trickle   B) deep   C) move   D) sneak

17. DOZE
A) amount   B) sleep   C) ease   D) nab

18. PROWL
A) hide   B) howl   C) lurk   D) roam

19. PRETENTIOUS
A) humble   B) natural   C) evil   D) showy

20. PREVAIL
A) win   B) forfeit   C) attack   D) gain

21. PRANCE
A) show   B) race   C) solidify   D) jump

22. CONTEMPLATE
A) decide   B) format   C) recollect   D) consider

23. UNASSUMING
A) straight   B) clear   C) modest   D) fickle

24. HECKLE
A) applaud   B) debate   C) assist   D) taunt

25. LEER
A) pick   B) lament   C) ogle   D) boo

26. QUAINT
A) odd   B) numerical   C) analytical   D) stable

SYNONYMS SET 7

Select the word that is closest in meaning to the capitalized word.

1. DISSIPATE
A) collect	B) educate	C) disperse	D) move

2. CONTRIVED
A) smooth	B) artificial	C) delivered	D) executed

3. ENTRAILS
A) expectations	B) bribes	C) intestines	D) gifts

4. ACCLAIM
A) announce	B) denounce	C) speak	D) praise

5. ILLUSTRIOUS
A) beautiful	B) distinguished	C) shiny	D) long

6. HELM
A) cap	B) control	C) hat	D) port

7. CREST
A) feature	B) peak	C) label	D) symbol

8. MARIONETTE
A) portrait	B) statue	C) puppet	D) mural

9. SUSTENANCE
A) lies	B) light	C) supplement	D) food

10. TERSE
A) nervous	B) strained	C) muted	D) abrupt

11. HARDIHOOD
A) empathy	B) skill	C) compassion	D) daring

12. PORTICO
A) window	B) porch	C) elevator	D) room

13. PREDICAMENT
A) foretelling   B) meeting   C) difficulty   D) guess

14. ENTOURAGE
A) troop   B) stimulus   C) pride   D) escort

15. CORROBORATE
A) erode   B) contradict   C) confuse   D) confirm

16. HUBBUB
A) habitat   B) center   C) noise   D) offense

17. CROSSROADS
A) clue   B) importance   C) turning point   D) terrain

18. SUBLIME
A) white   B) corrosive   C) excellent   D) famous

19. OBSCURE
A) reveal   B) explain   C) correct   D) conceal

20. ENCUMBER
A) count   B) split   C) restrict   D) release

21. FLAMBOYANT
A) pretty   B) modest   C) successful   D) flashy

22. PROVISIONAL
A) eatable   B) confirmed   C) illegal   D) temporary

23. CALLOW
A) slight   B) vigorous   C) immature   D) new

24. MISGIVING
A) query   B) sorrow   C) panic   D) doubt

25. ACUMEN
A) plan   B) skill   C) knowledge   D) thrift

26. MALICE
A) ill will   B) curiosity   C) intent   D) vengeance

SYNONYMS SET 8

Select the word that is closest in meaning to the capitalized word.

1. TYCOON
A) cyclone　　B) easterner　　C) magnet　　D) businessman

2. HAUGHTY
A) mischievous　　B) reclusive　　C) confident　　D) arrogant

3. BESTRIDE
A) beside　　B) walk　　C) mount　　D) gallop

4. EDIFICE
A) food　　B) structure　　C) frontage　　D) symbol

5. RUMINATE
A) consider　　B) enquire　　C) relate　　D) command

6. EPOCH
A) legend　　B) period　　C) tale　　D) epic

7. SWAGGER
A) swing　　B) bet　　C) strut　　D) swim

8. INUNDATE
A) begin　　B) propose　　C) deliver　　D) flood

9. CARESS
A) stroke　　B) celebrate　　C) consideration　　D) affection

10. SOVEREIGN
A) check　　B) rule　　C) idol　　D) king

11. RUE
A) remember　　B) note　　C) analyze　　D) regret

12. ESPY
A) bird　　B) hear　　C) see　　D) feel

13. SCRUTINIZE
A) deflect   B) examine   C) approve   D) threaten

14. JADED
A) dulled   B) related   C) green   D) decorated

15. VINDICATION
A) victory   B) justification   C) remembrance   D) conclusion

16. ACUITY
A) shortage   B) pride   C) sharpness   D) survey

17. SEQUESTER
A) arrange   B) pattern   C) imitate   D) isolate

18. TUMULT
A) swelling   B) sickness   C) tragedy   D) uproar

19. ORNERY
A) ordinary   B) routine   C) nasty   D) single

20. AUSPICIOUS
A) superstitious   B) agreeable   C) temporary   D) opportune

21. FEIGN
A) come down   B) rescue   C) pretend   D) remove

22. KNOLL
A) grass   B) hill   C) platform   D) garden

23. GENESIS
A) origin   B) divine   C) celestial   D) evolution

24. ACCOST
A) estimate   B) approach   C) bore   D) propose

25. ABSTRUSE
A) wide   B) adamant   C) puzzling   D) angular

26. ABSTEMIOUS
A) jealous   B) neutral   C) humble   D) moderate

SYNONYMS SET 9

Select the word that is closest in meaning to the capitalized word.

1. METICULOUS
A) careful   B) decorated   C) complete   D) enlarged

2. EUPHEMISM
A) description   B) explanation   C) insult   D) substitute

3. PRAGMATIC
A) ideal   B) skilled   C) practical   D) wise

4. VORACIOUS
A) loud   B) hungry   C) lively   D) eager

5. GERMANE
A) relevant   B) kind   C) refined   D) relative

6. ENIGMA
A) machine   B) puzzle   C) dilemma   D) trivia

7. BURNISH
A) provide   B) blacken   C) polish   D) dim

8. CAMOUFLAGE
A) green   B) uniform   C) match   D) disguise

9. MALODOROUS
A) ripe   B) fragrant   C) smelly   D) aromatic

10. WHIMSICAL
A) happy   B) fickle   C) rhythmic   D) picky

11. MOLLIFY
A) enrage   B) clarify   C) address   D) pacify

12. REPUDIATE
A) access   B) deprive   C) reject   D) withhold

13. INNOCUOUS
A) protective B) harmless C) dull D) tasteless

14. CONDONE
A) approve B) supervise C) contest D) consider

15. MILLINER
A) merchant B) hat maker C) tailor D) costumer

16. UTILITARIAN
A) certain B) specific C) practical D) spartan

17. APIARY
A) garden B) grove C) stable D) bee yard

18. RUSE
A) idea B) blend C) move D) trick

19. FLAUNT
A) teach B) discover C) predict D) show off

20. INSURGENT
A) flier B) criminal C) rebel D) deviant

21. APARTHEID
A) system B) segregation C) policy D) race

22. APPREHENSION
A) fear B) silence C) view D) hold

23. VIRULENT
A) bitter B) harmful C) numerous D) hard

24. ESPOUSE
A) debate B) discuss C) support D) dismiss

25. PALPABLE
A) visionary B) different C) flexible D) evident

26. FLOUNDER
A) stumble B) wander C) explore D) vary

SYNONYMS SET 10

Select the word that is closest in meaning to the capitalized word.

1. VOLATILE
A) angry B) unstable C) toxic D) negative

2. ABOMINABLE
A) ancient B) preventive C) huge D) horrible

3. ANTIPATHY
A) competition B) rivalry C) hatred D) curiosity

4. ABDICATE
A) anoint B) give up C) elevate D) transfer

5. LUCRATIVE
A) profitable B) attractive C) financial D) successful

6. TENACIOUS
A) hard B) persistent C) dense D) unsure

7. PARADIGM
A) plane B) technique C) example D) original

8. VIRTUOSO
A) story teller B) student C) teacher D) expert

9. ICONOCLAST
A) symbol B) idol worshipper C) rebel D) enemy

10. INSINUATION
A) hint B) inhaling C) comparison D) instruction

11. ZEALOT
A) follower B) insurgent C) disciple D) fanatic

12. VILIFY
A) acquire B) correct C) defame D) explain

13. SUPERFLUOUS
A) excellent   B) extra   C) comfortable   D) deep

14. PERMEATE
A) fill   B) allow   C) inject   D) violate

15. IGNOBLE
A) dumb   B) dishonorable   C) jealous   D) criminal

16. AGGRANDIZE
A) count   B) earn   C) magnify   D) display

17. MAVEN
A) beginner   B) stylist   C) consumer   D) expert

18. FLEDGLING
A) master   B) parent   C) fruit   D) beginner

19. BOLSTER
A) support   B) soften   C) gather   D) lost

20. SYNTHESIS
A) man made   B) product   C) addition   D) combination

21. BELLICOSE
A) numerous   B) reasonable   C) warlike   D) delayed

22. DEBILITATE
A) borrow   B) weaken   C) burden   D) obstruct

23. ABRASIVE
A) hard   B) polishing   C) corrosive   D) venomous

24. DEIGN
A) measure   B) concede   C) partner   D) refuse

25. TRITE
A) taut   B) dark   C) stale   D) precise

26. CONUNDRUM
A) logic   B) answer   C) adversity   D) riddle

SYNONYMS SET 11

Select the word that is closest in meaning to the capitalized word.

1. ADORN
A) decorate	B) analyze	C) exalt	D) elevate

2. SUBTLE
A) delicate	B) feeble	C) direct	D) persistent

3. PETITE
A) hungry	B) little	C) warm	D) childish

4. IMPERTINENT
A) essential	B) rude	C) angry	D) clever

5. VET
A) treat	B) handle	C) check	D) care

6. RANKLE
A) sort	B) arrange	C) irritate	D) remember

7. FROLIC
A) liberate	B) join	C) circle	D) play

8. ROUT
A) channel	B) track	C) reverse	D) defeat

9. SKULK
A) sneak	B) mop	C) stand	D) stare

10. CACKLE
A) burn	B) laugh	C) smile	D) roll

11. CAVORT
A) dance	B) hide	C) join	D) link

12. TROUNCE
A) defeat	B) dream	C) weight	D) play

13. ROMP
A) lesson   B) play   C) greed   D) display

14. ONEROUS
A) ordinary   B) laborious   C) disliked   D) united

15. LIVID
A) fatty   B) curious   C) angry   D) displeased

16. INSOLENCE
A) sleeplessness   B) gloom   C) disrespect   D) crankiness

17. BRAZEN
A) careless   B) tricky   C) loud   D) shameless

18. SASH
A) courage   B) cut   C) portion   D) waistband

19. PIDDLE
A) divide   B) dismiss   C) urinate   D) hesitate

20. OLFACTORY
A) sight   B) smell   C) sense   D) taste

21. IDIOSYNCRASY
A) quirk   B) pattern   C) unity   D) difference

22. STRADDLE
A) mount   B) horse   C) empty   D) lunge

23. VAGRANT
A) ruler   B) tramp   C) follower   D) criminal

24. ARMISTICE
A) appeal   B) truce   C) negotiation   D) purchase

25. MOTIF
A) aim   B) reason   C) design   D) tiff

26. PETULANT
A) angry   B) stubborn   C) irritable   D) hesitant

SYNONYMS SET 12

Select the word that is closest in meaning to the capitalized word.

1. EFFERVESCENT
A) bubbly B) aromatic C) placid D) still

2. PLUTOCRAT
A) millionaire B) astronaut C) dog walker D) villain

3. SALUTARY
A) respectful B) beneficial C) immediate D) enormous

4. ELUSIVE
A) fixed B) orphaned C) strict D) slippery

5. ILLICIT
A) unplanned B) illegal C) natural D) incomplete

6. IRRIGATE
A) anger B) water C) spread D) rise

7. ASKEW
A) aligned B) cornered C) wrong D) crooked

8. MIRTH
A) brightness B) noise C) bustle D) joy

9. IMPUGN
A) announce B) support C) challenge D) comment

10. INDIGO
A) rainbow B) hue C) blue D) paint

11. LADEN
A) loaded B) scooped C) weighed D) marked

12. GELATINOUS
A) gummy B) solid C) shiny D) opaque

13. SIFT
A) move   B) roam   C) filter   D) leak

14. REPROACH
A) blame   B) ban   C) sentence   D) advice

15. QUADRUPED
A) vehicle   B) animal   C) multiple   D) fraction

16. ENERVATE
A) boost   B) weaken   C) regulate   D) suck

17. SLOTHFUL
A) sad   B) dumb   C) deliberate   D) lazy

18. INCREDULOUS
A) fantastic   B) significant   C) endorsing   D) doubtful

19. SAUNTER
A) roll   B) gallop   C) stroll   D) slide

20. VAIN
A) strong   B) evil   C) proud   D) confident

21. CANTANKEROUS
A) grumpy   B) enraged   C) dependable   D) enlarged

22. EXTRICATE
A) rescue   B) eliminate   C) segregate   D) enmesh

23. UPROOT
A) elongate   B) pluck   C) plant   D) encourage

24. COGNIZANCE
A) influence   B) ignorance   C) awareness   D) oblivion

25. FATUOUS
A) obese   B) silly   C) testy   D) disunited

26. CLANDESTINE
A) legal   B) secretive   C) unknown   D) lonely

SYNONYMS SET 13

Select the word that is closest in meaning to the capitalized word.

1. CREDULOUS
A) naive	B) easy	C) suspicious	D) worldly

2. ACQUIESCE
A) inform	B) obtain	C) agree	D) acknowledge

3. ASSIMILATE
A) duplicate	B) defeat	C) demolish	D) absorb

4. REJUVENATE
A) return	B) reverse	C) restart	D) renew

5. CANOPY
A) leaf	B) tree	C) cover	D) obstacle

6. IGNEOUS
A) bent	B) variable	C) fiery	D) flexible

7. REVERBERATE
A) explain	B) echo	C) travel	D) refuse

8. GUFFAW
A) yawn	B) laugh	C) mistake	D) flaw

9. ULTIMATUM
A) demand	B) completion	C) ransom	D) announcement

10. UBIQUITOUS
A) universal	B) irritating	C) powerful	D) well read

11. ANTITHESIS
A) criticism	B) discussion	C) opposite	D) derivative

12. VERBIAGE
A) loud	B) wordiness	C) nonsensical	D) grammatical

13. DIMINUTIVE
A) precise   B) soft spoken   C) secretive   D) tiny

14. PROTEAN
A) gigantic   B) ancient   C) dogmatic   D) changeable

15. SPRITE
A) vigor   B) evil   C) fairy   D) life

16. ENCROACH
A) attempt   B) calculate   C) intrude   D) exit

17. DRUDGE
A) dirt   B) ground   C) slave   D) curse

18. RAMSHACKLE
A) enclosed   B) shaky   C) robust   D) sturdy

19. DEMARCATE
A) divide   B) symbolize   C) announce   D) reveal

20. REMUNERATION
A) wage   B) count   C) order   D) pattern

21. BEDLAM
A) agreement   B) movement   C) hostel   D) disorder

22. PERTURBATION
A) intrusion   B) disturbance   C) volatility   D) difficulty

23. MANTLE
A) helmet   B) throne   C) scepter   D) cloak

24. PRECIPITATE
A) expect   B) reject   C) demonstrate   D) cause

25. PRODIGAL
A) repentant   B) mistaken   C) wasteful   D) numerous

26. PROVOCATEUR
A) pioneer   B) forerunner   C) instigator   D) precursor

SYNONYMS SET 14

Select the word that is closest in meaning to the capitalized word.

1. FURTIVE
A) wealthy   B) illegal   C) sneaky   D) skillful

2. TRAILBLAZER
A) constructor   B) pioneer   C) researcher   D) rebel

3. TENTATIVE
A) uncertain   B) preliminary   C) unsound   D) wrinkled

4. PERUSE
A) chase   B) hear   C) read   D) learn

5. MENDICANT
A) trader   B) teacher   C) servant   D) beggar

6. CHAFF
A) chalk   B) rubbing   C) husk   D) impatience

7. PERNICIOUS
A) relevant   B) capricious   C) harmful   D) long lasting

8. CONFLUENCE
A) impact   B) junction   C) wealth   D) tributary

9. IMPLACABLE
A) restless   B) unappeasable   C) placable   D) motivated

10. KERNEL
A) compilation   B) skin   C) seed   D) absence

11. QUALM
A) help   B) thought   C) decision   D) regret

12. CIRCUMSPECT
A) complete   B) wary   C) confused   D) vivid

13. REBUKE
A) return	B) defeat	C) scold	D) explain

14. DWINDLE
A) erase	B) decrease	C) pile	D) handle

15. CONVALESCENCE
A) recovery	B) deterioration	C) infection	D) check

16. MYTHIC
A) mythical	B) long winded	C) bland	D) new

17. PRECIPITOUS
A) inducing	B) reasonable	C) filling	D) steep

18. PRUDENT
A) truthful	B) miserly	C) sparse	D) careful

19. APPRAISE
A) acclaim	B) recognize	C) assess	D) enable

20. PRETEXT
A) foreword	B) excuse	C) introduction	D) display

21. TUMULTUOUS
A) boring	B) fated	C) stormy	D) busy

22. CONFER
A) meet	B) discuss	C) give	D) agree

23. MALADY
A) treatment	B) poison	C) melody	D) disease

24. INCORRIGIBLE
A) flexible	B) hopeless	C) chaotic	D) quarrelsome

25. FLAGON
A) wine	B) pole	C) jug	D) bowel

26. LIMERICK
A) stone	B) poem	C) prayer	D) pamphlet

SYNONYMS SET 15

Select the word that is closest in meaning to the capitalized word.

1. TRUCULENT
A) combative   B) shy   C) pleased   D) cunning

2. PHILANTHROPY
A) charity   B) research   C) recovery   D) empathy

3. SERENE
A) blue   B) calm   C) wise   D) chill

4. HEADLONG
A) cautious   B) determined   C) stubborn   D) rash

5. ENCLAVE
A) cover   B) measure   C) territory   D) island

6. MAXIM
A) proverb   B) metaphor   C) simile   D) argument

7. WAIF
A) cub   B) orphan   C) nuisance   D) sapling

8. LEVITATE
A) travel   B) float   C) reduce   D) entertain

9. INTERDICT
A) standardize   B) dictate   C) intercept   D) ban

10. ACCOLADE
A) fame   B) premium   C) praise   D) treasure

11. SNARE
A) trap   B) survive   C) attack   D) call

12. APPARITION
A) movement   B) disappearance   C) mystery   D) ghost

13. DEBUT
A) preview   B) launch   C) prediction   D) initiative

14. ASCERTAIN
A) doubt   B) eliminate   C) guess   D) determine

15. LINGO
A) luck   B) language   C) spirit   D) assent

16. PAUCITY
A) lack   B) slowing   C) disturbance   D) distribution

17. IMPLICATE
A) comply   B) confuse   C) understand   D) incriminate

18. JARGON
A) vehicle   B) vernacular   C) jar   D) computer

19. JETTISON
A) accelerate   B) launch   C) glide   D) dump

20. CONFLAGRATION
A) meeting   B) debate   C) fire   D) prayer

21. TEMPERANCE
A) moderation   B) solution   C) understanding   D) delight

22. ANACHRONISTIC
A) repeated   B) outdated   C) variable   D) temporary

23. TEMPORAL
A) durable   B) worldly   C) countable   D) persistent

24. MULTITUDE
A) finite   B) skill   C) quantity   D) crowd

25. FLUMMOX
A) incite   B) flex   C) confuse   D) induce

26. VENAL
A) corrupt   B) thin   C) pained   D) wasteful

SYNONYMS SET 16

Select the word that is closest in meaning to the capitalized word.

1. ANOMALY
A) exception B) pattern C) information D) advantage

2. PARITY
A) equality B) division C) peeling D) stripping

3. STAUNCH
A) stop B) disloyal C) start D) pump

4. PLUMB
A) lower B) measure C) link D) align

5. ENDOWMENT
A) beauty B) gift C) strength D) offer

6. IMPECUNIOUS
A) routine B) poor C) simple D) innocent

7. SPORADIC
A) cyclical B) spherical C) irregular D) rhythmic

8. INDECOROUS
A) ugly B) decorum C) improper D) unexpected

9. CONTEMPORARY
A) known B) friendly C) modern D) fashionable

10. MAUSOLEUM
A) temple B) sanctuary C) statue D) tomb

11. IOTA
A) valve B) portion C) slice D) bit

12. DESIST
A) apologize B) slow C) continue D) abstain

13. SOBRIETY
A) seriousness B) restraint C) significance D) relevance

14. DETRIMENTAL
A) fragmented   B) harmful   C) disconnected   D) aiding

15. DIGRESS
A) deviate   B) concentrate   C) develop   D) explain

16. SUBVERT
A) undermine   B) dig   C) temper   D) separate

17. SUBJUGATE
A) overpower   B) undermine   C) address   D) administer

18. HARANGUE
A) tribute   B) tirade   C) eulogy   D) pray

19. PUERILE
A) unnecessary   B) childish   C) scarce   D) extinct

20. QUOTIDIAN
A) obedient   B) daily   C) occasional   D) essential

21. MUNDANE
A) regular   B) boring   C) musical   D) irritating

22. AMBLE
A) fill   B) hop   C) walk   D) track

23. PRATTLE
A) upset   B) boom   C) chatter   D) hum

24. INEBRIATED
A) burdened   B) worried   C) drunk   D) excited

25. POIGNANT
A) important   B) critical   C) elegant   D) moving

26. FORAGE
A) feast   B) fruit   C) travel   D) fodder

SYNONYMS SET 17

Select the word that is closest in meaning to the capitalized word.

1. CICATRIX
A) scar   B) worm   C) bird   D) branch

2. LACERATION
A) gap   B) blood   C) medicine   D) wound

3. TEMERITY
A) fear   B) moderation   C) nerve   D) skill

4. ADROIT
A) focused   B) clever   C) flexible   D) fit

5. NOTORIETY
A) disrepute   B) hatred   C) mismatch   D) avoidance

6. SUPPLE
A) plenty   B) pretty   C) flexible   D) desirable

7. REPREHENSIBLE
A) responsible B) avoidable   C) clueless   D) disgraceful

8. INDIGNATION
A) contentment B) irritation   C) resentment   D) satisfaction

9. DEPLORE
A) analyze   B) denounce   C) shun   D) demean

10. PEEVISH
A) irritable   B) frightened   C) disappointed D) expectant

11. AVID
A) steady   B) eager   C) anxious   D) nervous

12. DISCOURSE
A) walkway   B) complaint   C) letter   D) speech

13. BURGEON
A) lift B) attack C) increase D) burden

14. DERELICT
A) roaming B) abandoned C) gloomy D) finished

15. PRECIPICE
A) cliff B) bridge C) road D) slope

16. COMPATRIOT
A) friend B) coworker C) nationalist D) countryman

17. SEDITIOUS
A) filterable B) analytical C) censured D) disloyal

18. REIMBURSE
A) refuse B) refill C) repay D) rebuff

19. GAUNT
A) burned B) thin C) sad D) broken

20. EMACIATED
A) skinny B) decorated C) neglected D) empowered

21. CULINARY
A) arrangement B) hospitality C) nutrition D) cooking

22. ALLEGORY
A) accusation B) allege C) demonstration D) story

23. CONFIDANTE
A) guarantor B) sponsor C) friend D) patron

24. PLIABLE
A) salable B) impressionable C) strong D) mobile

25. COMPOSITE
A) blend B) product C) decay D) fission

26. SQUANDER
A) invest B) donate C) renounce D) waste

SYNONYMS SET 18

Select the word that is closest in meaning to the capitalized word.

1. INFAMY
A) disrepute	B) youth	C) corruption	D) gossip

2. SYNCOPATE
A) align	B) shorten	C) interpret	D) transcribe

3. DOCILE
A) tame	B) pleasant	C) pretty	D) direct

4. INDIGENOUS
A) angry	B) clever	C) native	D) annoyed

5. BAROQUE
A) insolvent	B) fancy	C) strict	D) bankrupt

6. ATTUNE
A) adjust	B) search	C) struggle	D) sympathize

7. SATIRE
A) clothing	B) theatre	C) expression	D) mockery

8. VILE
A) corrosive	B) clear	C) unpleasant	D) quick

9. NUANCED
A) compromised	B) refined	C) just	D) thoughtless

10. INSTIGATE
A) incite	B) examine	C) promote	D) vibrate

11. PICKLED
A) preserved	B) broken	C) tanned	D) boiled

12. CULPABLE
A) competent	B) eligible	C) selected	D) blamable

13. BELLIGERENT
A) fragile	B) respectful	C) hostile	D) repulsive

14. PARLANCE
A) weapon	B) language	C) background	D) field

15. SUBSIDIARY
A) secondary	B) reducing	C) relative	D) support

16. ACCRUE
A) collect	B) hint	C) plunder	D) donate

17. HACKNEYED
A) burdened	B) stale	C) unexpected	D) regular

18. PROFLIGATE
A) wasteful	B) shallow	C) outlier	D) foolish

19. BUSYBODY
A) celebrity	B) public figure	C) meddler	D) reformer

20. TRANSIENT
A) portable	B) temporary	C) unintended	D) erratic

21. PARODY
A) spoof	B) copy	C) adaptation	D) abridgment

22. PERVERSION
A) demolition	B) release	C) cleverness	D) corruption

23. INGRATIATING
A) sympathetic	B) uniting	C) flattering	D) thanking

24. FRISK
A) nervousness	B) search	C) elegance	D) adventure

25. EUPHORIA
A) happiness	B) aroma	C) relief	D) satisfaction

26. DIATRIBE
A) community	B) rant	C) buildup	D) crusade

SYNONYMS SET 19

Select the word that is closest in meaning to the capitalized word.

1. GRUELING
A) cooking B) continuous C) nutritious D) tiring

2. REVAMP
A) slope B) incline C) reduce D) rebuild

3. BESET
A) afflict B) earn C) lure D) attack

4. CALAMITOUS
A) complicated B) confusing C) dire D) linear

5. EXHILARATE
A) breathe B) extract C) dampen D) excite

6. VENEER
A) flesh B) facade C) meat D) overview

7. CURTAIL
A) cancel B) reduce C) revoke D) cover

8. BUTTRESS
A) fort B) defense C) support D) home

9. FLOUT
A) hate B) avoid C) endure D) defy

10. PALTRY
A) estimated B) little C) avian D) priceless

11. ARBITRATION
A) mediation B) selection C) administration D) pique

12. COGENT
A) manly B) logical C) unwanted D) winning

13. REVULSION
A) thrust B) tackiness C) disgust D) uprising

14. PROFUSE
A) calm B) lucky C) ancient D) abundant

15. FUTILE
A) inept B) delayed C) aimless D) pointless

16. RAVAGED
A) rotten B) damaged C) eliminated D) uncivilized

17. UNREPENTANT
A) proud B) evil C) zealous D) remorseless

18. ERRATIC
A) irregular B) circular C) recurring D) eventual

19. HAPHAZARD
A) dangerous B) callous C) random D) ugly

20. HOMAGE
A) service B) insult C) loan D) respect

21. OBLITERATE
A) rearrange B) fade C) disguise D) destroy

22. GUILE
A) cover B) cunning C) intelligence D) qualification

23. VERACITY
A) validity B) relevance C) truth D) confidence

24. PERFORATE
A) etch B) garnish C) scratch D) pierce

25. DISTEND
A) deflate B) flatten C) swell D) pretend

26. REPARATION
A) compensation B) restoration C) enhancement D) amendment

SYNONYMS SET 20

Select the word that is closest in meaning to the capitalized word.

1. ATROCITY
A) barbarity B) ugliness C) fraud D) immorality

2. GRIMY
A) bleak B) dirty C) smoky D) hopeless

3. ELOQUENCE
A) bombast B) dictation C) fluency D) extension

4. IMBUE
A) dry B) preach C) drain D) infuse

5. HONE
A) sharpen B) acquire C) blunt D) reply

6. TIFF
A) quarrel B) agreement C) dialogue D) competition

7. DISSUADE
A) agree B) prevent C) doctor D) argue

8. AVOW
A) deny B) concede C) declare D) argue

9. GARISH
A) drab B) covered C) obvious D) flashy

10. SCOFFLAW
A) lawyer B) policeman C) criminal D) judge

11. AESTHETIC
A) elegant B) sedative C) supernatural D) aromatic

12. PONDEROUS
A) thoughtful B) heavy C) worrisome D) silly

13. DEFERENTIAL
A) contrast   B) disparity   C) humble   D) aloof

14. MOROSE
A) cheerful   B) sullen   C) colorful   D) happy

15. SQUALID
A) dirty   B) round   C) fresh   D) square

16. PERPLEXED
A) confused   B) understanding   C) troubled   D) involved

17. APPENDAGE
A) addendum   B) index   C) faculty   D) replacement

18. DEXTERITY
A) cruelty   B) skill   C) rage   D) luck

19. PUGNACIOUS
A) smelly   B) ungainly   C) combative   D) acidic

20. BOUGH
A) division   B) stem   C) wave   D) branch

21. INOCULATION
A) ignorance   B) vaccination   C) warning   D) encouragement

22. SUFFRAGE
A) franchise   B) anger   C) movement   D) gathering

23. HISTRIONIC
A) ancient   B) dramatic   C) able   D) lazy

24. FATHOM
A) sell   B) clarify   C) understand   D) debate

25. BELITTLE
A) little   B) disparage   C) magnify   D) praise

26. SPURN
A) allocate   B) reciprocate   C) reject   D) appreciate

SYNONYMS SET 21

Select the word that is closest in meaning to the capitalized word.

1. ADMONISH
A) create B) adapt C) scold D) remove

2. PURGE
A) earn B) cleanse C) flow D) award

3. COWER
A) cringe B) run C) coat D) stand

4. PROFOUND
A) superficial B) helpful C) intense D) bad

5. VISAGE
A) visitor B) wisdom C) attraction D) expression

6. JURISDICTION
A) view B) balance C) authority D) research

7. RELINQUISH
A) achieve B) remake C) renounce D) reply

8. ITINERARY
A) bag B) route C) map D) location

9. EMBROIDERY
A) decoration B) cloth C) portrait D) color

10. FINESSE
A) health B) dedication C) skill D) timing

11. POSTERITY
A) behind B) bottom C) imagery D) descendants

12. HUSBANDRY
A) division B) relation C) farming D) evil

13. PORTRAITURE
A) color B) canvas C) description D) printer

14. EULOGY
A) scolding B) tribute C) agreement D) letter

15. LOQUACIOUS
A) talkative B) particular C) local D) indirect

16. FASTIDIOUS
A) quick B) fashionable C) particular D) accepting

17. GALE
A) laughter B) story C) ship D) storm

18. TANNER
A) leather-worker B) wood worker C) designer D) decorator

19. SQUALL
A) nail B) song C) storm D) boat

20. IGNOMINIOUS
A) victorious B) humiliating C) long lasting D) short

21. INCHOATE
A) rudimentary B) excellent C) dormant D) routine

22. INCARNATE
A) assist B) destroy C) represent D) convey

23. ACME
A) nadir B) poison C) peak D) liquid

24. SANCTION
A) separate B) argue C) learn D) approve

25. DETER
A) clear B) measure C) forgive D) prevent

26. AFFINITY
A) clarity B) enmity C) similarity D) eagerness

SYNONYMS SET 22

Select the word that is closest in meaning to the capitalized word.

1. FORLORN
   A) hopeless   B) dependable   C) feasible   D) smiling

2. HYPOCRITICAL
   A) insincere   B) important   C) trivial   D) analytical

3. PERILOUS
   A) dangerous   B) close   C) calm   D) predictable

4. APPROBATE
   A) fix   B) approve   C) think   D) match

5. SPEARHEAD
   A) destroy   B) lead   C) seek   D) develop

6. CUMBERSOME
   A) friendly   B) complex   C) quick   D) toxic

7. SINGULAR
   A) appreciative B) regular   C) unusual   D) appropriate

8. GLEAN
   A) cut   B) shine   C) gather   D) analyze

9. PESTER
   A) spread   B) control   C) bother   D) request

10. FLABBERGASTED
    A) defeated   B) decorated   C) eliminated D) astonished

11. FOOLHARDY
    A) strong   B) calculated   C) countering D) rash

12. CAPITULATE
    A) climb   B) stress   C) lead   D) surrender

13. MNEMONIC
A) disease B) vacuum C) reminder D) machine

14. PEDESTRIAN
A) boring B) motorist C) excellent D) rare

15. AMPLE
A) duplicate B) plenty C) avoidable D) simple

16. AVARICE
A) hatred B) compulsion C) separation D) greed

17. STOIC
A) heavy B) enclosed C) hungry D) impassive

18. ACRID
A) thick B) dark C) gaseous D) bitter

19. OBSTINATE
A) gastric B) irritable C) stubborn D) attractive

20. DIVULGE
A) distract B) destroy C) reveal D) differentiate

21. OVERSIGHT
A) research B) elimination C) supervision D) estimate

22. CONNIVE
A) greet B) plot C) celebrate D) attract

23. COMPENDIUM
A) organization B) collection C) pattern D) plan

24. PRESUMPTIVE
A) conclusive B) tentative C) spectacular D) effortless

25. FIASCO
A) failure B) painting C) result D) mural

26. OBLIGATION
A) duty B) ending C) permission D) discussion

SYNONYMS SET 23

Select the word that is closest in meaning to the capitalized word.

1. AMALGAMATION
A) combination   B) construction   C) result   D) fission

2. ROBUST
A) separate   B) sturdy   C) crumbling   D) precise

3. INDULGENT
A) tolerant   B) fancy   C) marked   D) nosy

4. PLUCK
A) learning   B) key   C) courage   D) interest

5. EMBLAZON
A) exclude   B) decorate   C) encourage   D) conquer

6. FIENDISH
A) wicked   B) noiseless   C) spotted   D) gentle

7. AMBIGUOUS
A) unbiased   B) energetic   C) average   D) vague

8. RESCIND
A) renew   B) conduct   C) cancel   D) impose

9. TOTEMIC
A) disturbed   B) symbolic   C) workable   D) ancient

10. HOLISTIC
A) entire   B) material   C) aspiring   D) riddled

11. PRECOCIOUS
A) tender   B) cute   C) advanced   D) illegal

12. ENDEMIC
A) obedient   B) harmless   C) lame   D) native

13. ARABLE
A) measurable   B) possible   C) fertile   D) feeble

14. BEGRUDGE
A) declare   B) envy   C) insert   D) deny

15. IMPERIOUS
A) arrogant   B) immense   C) generic   D) impartial

16. POROUS
A) penetrable   B) flippant   C) harsh   D) cowardly

17. DISPARAGE
A) deceive   B) insult   C) avoid   D) ignore

18. AMASS
A) gather   B) convince   C) indulge   D) approach

19. EXTOL
A) motivate   B) forgive   C) praise   D) snatch

20. BANTER
A) hearing   B) joke   C) relation   D) writing

21. PIQUANT
A) spicy   B) insipid   C) ruddy   D) tearful

22. BRANDISH
A) prosecute   B) throw   C) terminate   D) wave

23. IMPECCABLE
A) glistening   B) energetic   C) flawless   D) familiar

24. ENGROSS
A) etch   B) occupy   C) inflate   D) understand

25. PROLIFIC
A) productive   B) necessary   C) dynamic   D) huge

26. ENUNCIATE
A) pronounce   B) encourage   C) swear   D) inscribe

SYNONYMS SET 24

Select the word that is closest in meaning to the capitalized word.

1. BOMBASTIC
A) giddy   B) damaging   C) exotic   D) pompous

2. INFLUX
A) record   B) growth   C) treatment   D) inflow

3. RECONCILE
A) study   B) settle   C) remain   D) achieve

4. SWARTHY
A) mixed   B) handy   C) dark   D) clever

5. INSCRUTABLE
A) successful   B) responsible   C) hospitable   D) mysterious

6. INCAPACITATE
A) disable   B) imitate   C) handle   D) contribute

7. TORRID
A) adamant   B) alcoholic   C) sneaky   D) hot

8. PLATEAUED
A) destroyed   B) conserved   C) flattened   D) obstructed

9. AMBIVALENCE
A) distribution   B) uncertainty   C) direction   D) experience

10. POTENT
A) powerful   B) regular   C) tasteless   D) perfect

11. TENUOUS
A) entertaining   B) weak   C) dependent   D) stupid

12. APPARATUS
A) design   B) rainstorm   C) equipment   D) representative

13. MACE
A) toxin B) club C) cloth D) magic

14. CANTATA
A) volcano B) caption C) music D) development

15. ADHERE
A) identify B) assort C) surround D) follow

16. NONPLUSSED
A) constrained B) confused C) pretended D) challenged

17. GARRISON
A) troops B) cleave C) submit D) magnify

18. ODYSSEY
A) reward B) journey C) ship D) punishment

19. PATENT
A) careful B) obvious C) decisive D) steady

20. CANDOR
A) boundary B) honesty C) peace D) thrill

21. CUPIDITY
A) friction B) aversion C) greed D) existence

22. GOAD
A) hinder B) welcome C) provoke D) display

23. JAUNT
A) establishment B) trip C) smash D) flavor

24. QUAGMIRE
A) earthquake B) mess C) cluster D) afterthought

25. SPURIOUS
A) shallow B) guarded C) selective D) fake

26. COUNTERFEIT
A) reply B) revenge C) crime D) fake

SYNONYMS SET 25

Select the word that is closest in meaning to the capitalized word.

1. QUINTESSENTIAL
A) typical   B) productive   C) unusual   D) enchanted

2. INDUBITABLE
A) uptight   B) sure   C) domineering   D) powerful

3. ACRIMONY
A) surprise   B) bitterness   C) statement   D) produce

4. INTREPID
A) festive   B) concerned   C) obnoxious   D) fearless

5. GESTICULATION
A) range   B) knowledge   C) signal   D) attraction

6. FALLOW
A) inactive   B) dynamic   C) faint   D) ugly

7. VICARIOUS
A) strange   B) flowery   C) melodic   D) indirect

8. SPECK
A) dock   B) bit   C) fight   D) stream

9. STAGNATE
A) salute   B) implicate   C) consult   D) languish

10. STATURE
A) business   B) agreement   C) reputation   D) experience

11. STEADFAST
A) loyal   B) cheerful   C) graceful   D) comfortable

12. SUCCINCT
A) convincing   B) thorough   C) compact   D) pathetic

13. SULLY
A) value B) taint C) guide D) squeeze

14. SURROGATE
A) friend B) addition C) relation D) substitute

15. TAPER
A) frame B) freeze C) reduce D) delete

16. TAUNT
A) insult B) heave C) infest D) pacify

17. TERSE
A) familiar B) scattered C) clipped D) fascinated

18. TRIFLE
A) striped B) trivial C) wicked D) childlike

19. THWART
A) provide B) astonish C) dispose D) prevent

20. UNCOUTH
A) tender B) slippery C) crude D) fearful

21. VEND
A) sell B) thrive C) operate D) spit

22. UNRULY
A) disastrous B) wild C) exclusive D) doubtful

23. VERSATILE
A) literate B) all-round C) selective D) functional

24. VIBRANT
A) immense B) vengeful C) maniacal D) lively

25. VIGOROUS
A) glorious B) optimal C) strong D) precious

26. VOYAGE
A) journey B) trade C) exchange D) transport

SYNONYMS SET 26

Select the word that is closest in meaning to the capitalized word.

1. WANE
A) charge B) decrease C) enlarge D) distribute

2. WRITHE
A) wriggle B) transform C) screw D) insert

3. ZANY
A) curvy B) inconclusive C) peculiar D) bright

4. PREREQUISITE
A) observation B) essential C) adjustment D) agreement

5. BOORISH
A) rude B) idiotic C) crooked D) sudden

6. EXPEDITE
A) resist B) prepare C) violate D) speed up

7. TRANQUIL
A) magical B) obedient C) peaceful D) enthusiastic

8. COMMEND
A) send B) praise C) convene D) include

9. DELIRIOUS
A) raving B) talented C) righteous D) accidental

10. VESTIGE
A) respect B) remainder C) destruction D) activity

11. COLLUSION
A) request B) operation C) statement D) plot

12. AMNESTY
A) boon B) purpose C) pardon D) belief

13. STERLING
A) ancient B) excellent C) interesting D) reflective

14. BRUNT
A) impact B) battle C) harbor D) memory

15. LIMPID
A) slow B) clear C) marked D) late

16. EBB
A) retreat B) impend C) stride D) originate

17. WHEEDLE
A) upset B) injure C) persuade D) transfer

18. UNLETTERED
A) uninterested B) illiterate C) dogmatic D) disgusting

19. SOJOURN
A) stay B) flavor C) attempt D) theory

20. ILLUMINE
A) astonish B) announce C) stimulate D) brighten

21. AGOG
A) gloomy B) confused C) excited D) hapless

22. HIGHWAYMAN
A) patrolman B) robber C) guard D) driver

23. MERRIMENT
A) fun B) attraction C) shame D) hearing

24. IGNOBLE
A) defeated B) unworthy C) taboo D) defeated

25. DISDAIN
A) tendency B) regret C) suggestion D) contempt

26. TORMENT
A) protest B) thought C) suffering D) limit

SYNONYMS SET 27

Select the word that is closest in meaning to the capitalized word.

1. LARK
A) scent B) comfort C) breath D) fun

2. SOLEMNITY
A) design B) development C) request D) dignity

3. LEADEN
A) rampant B) futuristic C) heavy D) fluttering

4. VITALITY
A) friction B) pleasure C) insurance D) life

5. PRUDE
A) tinkerer B) moralist C) optimist D) pessimist

6. BEARING
A) station B) manner C) walk D) roaring

7. INTERMINABLE
A) unbiased B) unsuitable C) endless D) superficial

8. NADIR
A) exchange B) trade C) middle D) bottom

9. PANOPLY
A) color B) approval C) display D) linen

10. INTRANSIGENT
A) stubborn B) disturbed C) doubtful D) frightened

11. MUSLIN
A) mask B) cloth C) channel D) stream

12. PARASOL
A) helmet B) companion C) umbrella D) shadow

13. SALLOW
A) rigid	B) unique	C) abrupt	D) pale

14. FEISTY
A) selective	B) impartial	C) possessive	D) spirited

15. OMNIBUS
A) treasure	B) precise	C) rarity	D) collection

16. FRAIL
A) shallow	B) grey	C) weak	D) dusty

17. FORMIDABLE
A) decisive	B) gruesome	C) mighty	D) glorious

18. SONOROUS
A) funny	B) truthful	C) voiceless	D) booming

19. OMINOUS
A) threatening	B) crazy	C) shrill	D) energetic

20. TRANSFIXED
A) surrounded	B) mesmerized	C) shattered	D) forgot

21. RAMPART
A) location	B) interior	C) fortification	D) carriage

22. SMITTEN
A) sloppy	B) married	C) muddled	D) charmed

23. CONCORD
A) agreement	B) speed	C) advancement	D) collect

24. GENTRY
A) upper class	B) guard	C) committee	D) drain

25. EXONERATE
A) forget	B) clear	C) arrange	D) contrast

26. IMPERATIVE
A) slippery	B) huge	C) essential	D) permanent

SYNONYMS SET 28

Select the word that is closest in meaning to the capitalized word.

1. BRAMBLE
A) blackberry B) fight C) money D) tooth

2. MINCE
A) cut up B) tremble C) restrain D) shock

3. QUERULOUS
A) jealous B) whiny C) deafening D) aggressive

4. FRIVOLOUS
A) outgoing B) silly C) evasive D) combative

5. INDOMITABLE
A) flawless B) delightful C) brave D) puzzling

6. GAIETY
A) anger B) thought C) cheer D) vacation

7. LANGUOR
A) surprise B) sorrow C) excitement D) laziness

8. ZEPHYR
A) ship B) horizon C) spring D) breeze

9. WHIMSY
A) quiet B) fancy C) maid D) swing

10. ESCAPADE
A) accident B) meeting C) crash D) prank

11. EVANESCENT
A) bubbly B) scary C) melodious D) fading

12. TAWNY
A) feline B) flexible C) cuddly D) brown

13. BENIGNANT
A) harmful B) serious C) kind D) surprising

14. SPECTRAL
A) skillful B) proud C) ghostly D) nifty

15. CRAVEN
A) necessary B) coward C) sore D) wary

16. CAROUSE
A) care B) revel C) believe D) contest

17. PROFFER
A) offer B) earn C) praise D) differ

18. INFIRMITY
A) weakness B) stretch C) industry D) shame

19. AUGUST
A) original B) distinguished C) loving D) romantic

20. PROSTRATE
A) living B) flat C) dull D) superior

21. KOWTOW
A) discuss B) conspire C) grovel D) argue

22. BALLYHOO
A) shame B) preparation C) hype D) protest

23. MANUMIT
A) develop B) agree C) select D) free

24. CASTIGATE
A) apply B) allocate C) eliminate D) scold

25. NEOPHYTE
A) beginner B) consumer C) replacement D) modernist

26. INTERLOPER
A) mediator B) trespasser C) caretaker D) judge

SYNONYMS SET 29

Select the word that is closest in meaning to the capitalized word.

1. JUXTAPOSE
A) derive
B) import
C) inflate
D) compare

2. GENTILITY
A) reaction
B) attraction
C) connection
D) respectability

3. MORBID
A) cheap
B) magnificent
C) horrible
D) faulty

4. ODIOUS
A) heavenly
B) disgusting
C) bright
D) dramatic

5. HALCYON
A) pleasant
B) witty
C) strange
D) special

6. IMPART
A) submit
B) give
C) yell
D) blow

7. GIRD
A) compete
B) rebuild
C) encircle
D) spread

8. PANEGYRIC
A) payment
B) health
C) discussion
D) tribute

9. HEINOUS
A) uptight
B) puzzled
C) evil
D) planned

10. METTLE
A) reason
B) need
C) amount
D) fortitude

11. OBNOXIOUS
A) faded
B) disastrous
C) unpleasant
D) helpless

12. PINION
A) summon
B) restrain
C) collect
D) drag

13. IMPEDE
A) hinder B) innovate C) notify D) select

14. GLOWER
A) admire B) glare C) announce D) betray

15. INCENDIARY
A) slippery B) hospitable C) provocative D) lethal

16. HERALD
A) impress B) permit C) ribald D) announce

17. MORTIFICATION
A) income B) connection C) suggestion D) shame

18. OBLIQUE
A) puzzling B) grumpy C) tired D) indirect

19. IMPETUOUS
A) better B) beneficial C) impulsive D) longing

20. LEXICON
A) pattern B) dictionary C) announcement D) request

21. GLUT
A) surplus B) hope C) balance D) riddle

22. QUENCH
A) freeze B) satisfy C) detect D) ignore

23. INDOLENT
A) rough B) coherent C) lazy D) upbeat

24. MAWKISH
A) needless B) infamous C) unusual D) overemotional

25. GOVERNESS
A) ruler B) minister C) nanny D) manager

26. RAPACIOUS
A) glossy B) gaping C) noisy D) greedy

SYNONYMS SET 30

Select the word that is closest in meaning to the capitalized word.

1. LILTING
A) musical	B) beneficial	C) glistening	D) friendly

2. PRIMORDIAL
A) defiant	B) primitive	C) boundless	D) fearless

3. MENDACIOUS
A) ruthless	B) shallow	C) lying	D) hulking

4. HUMBUG
A) kettle	B) hive	C) death	D) hoax

5. MITIGATION
A) irritation	B) connection	C) observation	D) reduction

6. GLUTTONOUS
A) excited	B) stimulating	C) disturbed	D) greedy

7. LAMPOON
A) apologize	B) indicate	C) mock	D) press

8. PATHOS
A) shame	B) poignancy	C) prison	D) comfort

9. HYPERBOLE
A) exaggeration	B) trickery	C) criticism	D) literature

10. GRATIS
A) thin	B) free	C) polite	D) aloof

11. HEW
A) supply	B) detect	C) cut	D) sort

12. MISNOMER
A) competition	B) destruction	C) idea	D) misnaming

13. PERIPATETIC
A) diabetic
B) medicinal
C) wandering
D) vulnerable

14. MALCONTENT
A) partner
B) trade
C) ruin
D) troublemaker

15. INFALLIBLE
A) rigid
B) unsuitable
C) flawless
D) abundant

16. JABBER
A) zipper
B) chatter
C) weapon
D) request

17. PARTISAN
A) supporter
B) architect
C) announcer
D) onlooker

18. IMPLORE
A) belong
B) beg
C) install
D) stray

19. PERPETRATOR
A) follower
B) criminal
C) mediator
D) announcer

20. JEAPORDIZE
A) spread
B) expect
C) risk
D) earn

21. JOCUND
A) alert
B) violent
C) careful
D) happy

22. PINNACLE
A) bottom
B) peak
C) humor
D) title

23. MONOTONOUS
A) particular
B) singular
C) uneven
D) boring

24. INTOXICATED
A) poisoned
B) alert
C) drunk
D) capable

25. PARAGON
A) wax
B) embodiment
C) opposite
D) indent

26. INIMICAL
A) harmful
B) distinct
C) elastic
D) triple

Synonyms - Answers

Set 1		_Set 2_		_Set 3_		_Set 4_		_Set 5_	
Q No.	Answer	Q No.	Answer	Q No.	Answer	Q No.	Answer	Q No.	Answer
1	A	1	A	1	B	1	A	1	A
2	B	2	B	2	B	2	B	2	B
3	C	3	C	3	C	3	C	3	C
4	D	4	D	4	D	4	C	4	D
5	D	5	A	5	D	5	B	5	C
6	D	6	B	6	B	6	B	6	A
7	D	7	B	7	B	7	B	7	D
8	C	8	B	8	B	8	C	8	C
9	D	9	D	9	D	9	D	9	D
10	D	10	D	10	C	10	A	10	B
11	A	11	A	11	B	11	A	11	A
12	B	12	C	12	C	12	B	12	B
13	C	13	D	13	C	13	C	13	C
14	D	14	C	14	B	14	D	14	D
15	A	15	A	15	A	15	B	15	D
16	C	16	A	16	A	16	A	16	A
17	B	17	B	17	B	17	B	17	D
18	C	18	C	18	D	18	C	18	C
19	D	19	D	19	D	19	B	19	D
20	C	20	B	20	D	20	C	20	B
21	A	21	A	21	A	21	C	21	B
22	B	22	B	22	B	22	B	22	B
23	C	23	C	23	C	23	C	23	C
24	D	24	B	24	D	24	D	24	D
25	B	25	B	25	D	25	C	25	A
26	A	26	B	26	A	26	A	26	A

SYNONYMS - ANSWERS

Set 6		Set 7		Set 8		Set 9		Set 10	
Q No.	Answer	Q No.	Answer	Q No.	Answer	Q No.	Answer	Q No.	Answer
1	A	1	C	1	D	1	A	1	B
2	B	2	B	2	D	2	D	2	D
3	C	3	C	3	C	3	C	3	C
4	D	4	D	4	B	4	B	4	B
5	D	5	B	5	A	5	A	5	A
6	B	6	B	6	B	6	B	6	B
7	B	7	B	7	C	7	C	7	C
8	C	8	C	8	D	8	D	8	D
9	D	9	D	9	A	9	C	9	C
10	C	10	D	10	D	10	B	10	A
11	C	11	D	11	D	11	D	11	D
12	B	12	B	12	C	12	C	12	C
13	C	13	C	13	B	13	B	13	B
14	D	14	D	14	A	14	A	14	A
15	B	15	D	15	B	15	B	15	B
16	A	16	C	16	C	16	C	16	C
17	B	17	C	17	D	17	D	17	D
18	C	18	C	18	D	18	D	18	D
19	D	19	D	19	C	19	D	19	A
20	A	20	C	20	D	20	C	20	D
21	D	21	D	21	C	21	B	21	C
22	D	22	D	22	B	22	A	22	B
23	C	23	C	23	A	23	B	23	C
24	D	24	D	24	B	24	C	24	B
25	C	25	B	25	C	25	D	25	C
26	A	26	A	26	D	26	A	26	D

SYNONYMS - ANSWERS

Set 11		Set 12		Set 13		Set 14		Set 15	
Q No.	Answer	Q No.	Answer	Q No.	Answer	Q No.	Answer	Q No.	Answer
1	A	1	A	1	A	1	C	1	A
2	A	2	A	2	C	2	B	2	A
3	B	3	B	3	D	3	A	3	B
4	B	4	D	4	D	4	C	4	D
5	C	5	B	5	C	5	D	5	C
6	C	6	B	6	C	6	C	6	A
7	D	7	D	7	B	7	C	7	B
8	D	8	D	8	B	8	B	8	B
9	A	9	C	9	A	9	B	9	D
10	B	10	C	10	A	10	C	10	C
11	A	11	A	11	C	11	D	11	A
12	A	12	A	12	B	12	B	12	D
13	B	13	C	13	D	13	C	13	B
14	B	14	A	14	D	14	B	14	D
15	C	15	B	15	C	15	A	15	B
16	C	16	B	16	C	16	A	16	A
17	D	17	D	17	C	17	D	17	D
18	D	18	D	18	B	18	D	18	B
19	C	19	C	19	A	19	C	19	D
20	B	20	C	20	A	20	B	20	C
21	A	21	A	21	D	21	C	21	A
22	A	22	A	22	B	22	C	22	B
23	B	23	B	23	D	23	D	23	B
24	B	24	C	24	D	24	B	24	D
25	C	25	B	25	C	25	C	25	C
26	C	26	B	26	C	26	B	26	A

SYNONYMS - ANSWERS

Set 16		Set 17		Set 18		Set 19		Set 20	
Q No.	Answer	Q No.	Answer	Q No.	Answer	Q No.	Answer	Q No.	Answer
1	A	1	A	1	A	1	D	1	A
2	A	2	D	2	B	2	D	2	B
3	A	3	C	3	A	3	A	3	C
4	B	4	B	4	C	4	C	4	D
5	B	5	A	5	B	5	D	5	A
6	B	6	C	6	A	6	B	6	A
7	C	7	D	7	D	7	B	7	B
8	C	8	C	8	C	8	C	8	C
9	C	9	B	9	B	9	D	9	D
10	D	10	A	10	A	10	B	10	C
11	D	11	B	11	A	11	A	11	A
12	D	12	D	12	D	12	B	12	B
13	A	13	C	13	C	13	C	13	C
14	B	14	B	14	B	14	D	14	B
15	A	15	A	15	A	15	D	15	A
16	A	16	D	16	A	16	B	16	A
17	A	17	D	17	B	17	D	17	A
18	B	18	C	18	A	18	A	18	B
19	B	19	B	19	C	19	C	19	C
20	B	20	A	20	B	20	D	20	D
21	B	21	D	21	A	21	D	21	B
22	C	22	D	22	D	22	B	22	A
23	C	23	C	23	C	23	C	23	B
24	C	24	B	24	B	24	D	24	C
25	D	25	A	25	A	25	C	25	B
26	D	26	D	26	B	26	A	26	C

SYNONYMS - ANSWERS

Set 21		Set 22		Set 23		Set 24		Set 25	
Q No.	Answer	Q No.	Answer	Q No.	Answer	Q No.	Answer	Q No.	Answer
1	C	1	A	1	A	1	D	1	A
2	B	2	A	2	B	2	D	2	B
3	A	3	A	3	A	3	B	3	B
4	C	4	B	4	C	4	C	4	D
5	D	5	B	5	B	5	D	5	C
6	C	6	B	6	A	6	A	6	A
7	C	7	C	7	D	7	D	7	D
8	B	8	C	8	C	8	C	8	B
9	A	9	C	9	B	9	B	9	D
10	C	10	D	10	A	10	A	10	C
11	D	11	D	11	C	11	B	11	A
12	C	12	D	12	D	12	C	12	C
13	C	13	C	13	C	13	B	13	B
14	B	14	A	14	B	14	C	14	D
15	A	15	B	15	A	15	D	15	C
16	C	16	D	16	A	16	B	16	A
17	D	17	D	17	B	17	A	17	C
18	A	18	D	18	A	18	B	18	B
19	C	19	C	19	C	19	B	19	D
20	B	20	C	20	B	20	B	20	C
21	A	21	C	21	A	21	C	21	A
22	C	22	B	22	D	22	C	22	B
23	C	23	B	23	C	23	B	23	B
24	D	24	B	24	B	24	B	24	D
25	D	25	A	25	A	25	D	25	C
26	C	26	A	26	A	26	D	26	A

SYNONYMS - ANSWERS

Set 26		Set 27		Set 28		Set 29		Set 30	
Q No.	Answer	Q No.	Answer	Q No.	Answer	Q No.	Answer	Q No.	Answer
1	B	1	D	1	A	1	D	1	A
2	A	2	D	2	A	2	D	2	B
3	C	3	C	3	B	3	C	3	C
4	B	4	D	4	B	4	B	4	D
5	A	5	B	5	C	5	A	5	D
6	D	6	B	6	C	6	B	6	D
7	C	7	C	7	D	7	C	7	C
8	B	8	D	8	D	8	D	8	B
9	A	9	C	9	B	9	C	9	A
10	B	10	A	10	D	10	D	10	B
11	D	11	B	11	D	11	C	11	C
12	C	12	C	12	D	12	B	12	D
13	B	13	D	13	C	13	A	13	C
14	A	14	D	14	C	14	B	14	D
15	B	15	D	15	B	15	C	15	C
16	A	16	C	16	B	16	D	16	B
17	C	17	C	17	A	17	D	17	A
18	B	18	D	18	A	18	D	18	B
19	A	19	A	19	B	19	C	19	B
20	D	20	B	20	B	20	B	20	C
21	C	21	C	21	C	21	A	21	D
22	B	22	D	22	C	22	B	22	B
23	A	23	A	23	D	23	C	23	D
24	B	24	A	24	D	24	D	24	C
25	D	25	B	25	A	25	C	25	B
26	C	26	C	26	B	26	D	26	A

Made in the USA
Monee, IL
19 September 2021